Also by David Fischer:

A Yankee Stadium Scrapbook
Smithsonian Q & A Baseball
Greatest Sports Rivalries
Sports of the Times
The Encyclopedia of the Summer Olympics
The Story of the New York Yankees
Baseball Top 10
A Thing or Two About Baseball
Do Curve Balls Really Curve?
The 50 Coolest Jobs in Sports
Roberto Clemente: Trailblazer of the Modern World
Albert Pujols
Alex Rodriguez
Babe Ruth: Legendary Slugger

Cool Sports Dad

75 Amazing
Sporting Tricks to
Teach and Impress
Your Kids

DAVID FISCHER

Illustrations by
Adam Wallenta

Skyhorse Publishing

Skyhorse Publishing books may be purchased in bulk at special discounts for sales promotion, corporate gifts, fund-raising, or educational purposes. Special editions can also be created to specifications. For details, contact Special Sales Department, Skyhorse Publishing, 555 Eighth Avenue, Suite 903, New York, NY 10018 or info@skyhorsepublishing.com.

Library of Congress Cataloging-in-Publication data is available on file.
ISBN: 978-1-60239-965-5

Printed in China

To Rachel and Jack,

Thanks for always letting me play, too.

Love,
Dad

CONTENTS

INTRODUCTION

Of all the reasons why dads want their kids to play sports, the most important reason is to have fun. But some sports are difficult games to play and their skills are not always easy to understand and master. So what does a dad say to his youngster when he asks how to choose the right baseball bat? Or when she wants to know how to spike a volleyball? Or when you are asked to explain how to skip a stone across water?

Relax! This is where *Cool Sports Dad* can save the day. In this book, you will find lots of instructional guidance from famous professional athletes who have excelled over the years. You'll also find the basic fundamentals of sports explained by legendary coaches. And you'll find lots of time-tested tips and how to apply them so that your young athlete will get the most from the game. Of course, there's also plenty of solid advice on everything from how to break in a new baseball glove to how to toss a Frisbee. This book is intended for dads who want to help their children learn some of the basic skills of their favorite sports. It will help your child overcome the obstacles and experience the pleasures of participating in youth athletics, whether in an organized league or at the schoolyard with friends or in the backyard alone.

This book covers more than twenty sports. Open to any page, and you'll discover something about playing games you never knew before. Fascinate your kids by juggling three balls in the air, dazzle them with a lesson in how to throw a football with a perfect spiral, and amaze them with tips on how to snag a foul ball at a major-league baseball game—plus a whole lot more.

Baseball

Choosing the Right Baseball Bat

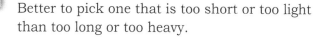

DAVID WRIGHT
Four-time MLB All-Star

Quick Tip

Better to pick one that is too short or too light than too long or too heavy.

① Most professional players now use light bats that weigh about 33 ounces to maintain bat speed, which is the top priority in hitting. Youngsters use bats that are significantly smaller (see sidebar). However, it's still crucial that an inexperienced player have a light bat to swing. This gives a player enough bat speed to hit the ball with authority. "A young player needs to learn to make contact with the ball and hit close to the 'sweet spot' of the bat," says Wright, who has a .311 career batting average since entering the major leagues with the New York Mets in 2004.

② Most organized leagues supply each team with a number of bats. When your child selects a bat, it's better to pick one that is too short or too light than too heavy or too long. The bat's handle, or grip, should not be too wide. "A thinner handle provides increased bat speed," says Wright, winner of the Silver Slugger award as the best-hitting third baseman in the National League in 2007 and 2008.

③ Make sure your child can handle the bat he wants before you buy it. A player should be able to handle a bat that can be held straight out in front (or to the side) with one hand at the knob for 25 seconds.

④ Before buying a bat, have your child hit with a selection of bats supplied by the league. You'll see right away which ones are too small, too big, or too heavy. Says Wright:

"With a bat that is an inch or two too long, the player might choke up a little." If he needs to choke up more than an inch, however, go to the next inch-size down.

⑤ Before you decide to purchase a bat for your child, ask your league about any limits on bat size or weight.

 David Wright finished second to Ryan Howard in the 2006 All-Star Game Home Run Derby.

Size Matters

Worth, the bat manufacturer, commissioned a research project to determine the best bat weight for players in youth baseball. The company developed a formula that divides the player's height in inches by four and adds four.

(Height ÷ 4) + 4 = Best Bat Weight
8–10 Years Old

Player Height	Best Bat Weight
48 inches	16 ounces
52 inches	17 ounces
56 inches	18 ounces
60 inches	19 ounces

As kids age, Worth suggests, use weight instead of height to select the best bat weight. The formula divides the player's weight in pounds by 18 and adds 14.

(Weight ÷ 18) + 14 = Best Bat Weight
11–12 Years Old

Player Weight	Best Bat Weight
80 pounds	19 ounces
100 pounds	20 ounces
120 pounds	21 ounces
140 pounds	22 ounces

Choosing a Baseball Glove

NOMAR GARCIAPARRA
Six-time MLB All-Star

Make sure the glove feels comfortable and fits your hand well.

① Go to sporting goods stores and try on several different gloves. Try not to be influenced by "autographs" of famous players.

② Remember that buying a glove is like buying a pair of shoes. The item should feel good when worn, and it will become more comfortable as it softens from use. "I used the same glove through high school," says Garciaparra, the 1997 American League Rookie of the Year.

③ The fielder must be able to move the glove quickly to the ball. This requires a glove that's not too big and not too heavy. You must be able to close the glove with your hand so that the ball does not pop out.

④ When choosing a particular glove, test it to make sure the glove is not too loose. Place a ball in the webbing and hold the baseball in the glove with the palm facing downward. If the ball falls to the floor, select a smaller model.

⑤ The glove should be in proportion to the player's hand. Balls will be harder to control with a bigger glove. Buy the smallest glove that will do the job properly for the player. The increase in glove control far outweighs the advantage of more reach.

⑥ More expensive is not always better when it comes to baseball gloves. "My father bought me a glove for $125, which our family really couldn't afford," Garciaparra recalls. "So I made sure it would last and took care of it." Players just starting out will do fine with vinyl or combination vinyl and leather models. These are less expensive than leather

and have pockets that bend and flex easily, giving greater glove control to small children or those with limited strength.

⑦ Garciaparra won two consecutive American League batting championships in 1999 and 2000, but he knows it is a fielder's glove that is a player's most irreplaceable piece of equipment. "You've got to respect your gear," he says. "I never throw my glove. I place it down in the dugout."

Nomar Garciaparra has played shortstop, third base, and first base for four major-league teams since 1996.

Breaking in a New Glove

DENNY WHITESIDE

Glove Engineer, Rawlings Sporting Goods Company

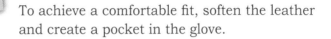

To achieve a comfortable fit, soften the leather and create a pocket in the glove.

① There are many different methods for breaking in a new baseball glove. Every player has his own ritual, and each will staunchly defend this method as the best. No matter the preferred method, the goal is to make the glove as comfortable as possible on your hand, until it fits like, um, a glove.

② Brand-new baseball gloves are pretty stiff, so the first thing you need to do is soften up the leather. Besides playing catch or spending hours throwing a ball into your glove, there are a number of different creams, oils, and lotions that can be used to soften the leather of your glove. The most popular include baby oil, mink oil, petroleum jelly, foam shaving cream, and saddle soap. To be sure, all the major glove manufacturers peddle their own magical concoction.

③ Whatever lotion or potion you decide to use, never over-lubricate your glove. Whiteside recommends using a clean cloth and working a small dollop of foam shaving cream with lanolin into the palm of your glove. "This will ensure that your glove stays soft while adding a layer of protection," he says. Be sure to rub the foam completely into the leather, paying specific attention to the glove's flex points. This will help reduce the stiffness of the new leather. Don't ignore the laces or hard-to-get-to areas. With a clean rag, wipe off any excess moisture.

④ To achieve a comfortable fit, you need to soften the leather and create a pocket in the glove. The pocket of the glove is the space between your thumb and forefinger. A well-formed pocket makes

catching baseballs or softballs much easier. Place a baseball or softball in the pocket of the glove and fold it closed. This will allow for your glove to more readily conform to the shape of a baseball. Wrap your glove with large rubber bands, twine, string, shoelaces, or a belt. Don't store a wrapped glove under your mattress. "Let it rest in a cool, dry place," says Whiteside, who has spent the past eighteen years as a glove project engineer in research and development at the sporting goods company's St. Louis headquarters.

⑤ Never place your glove under the tire of a car, as this will flatten the glove. "Yes, people do this," says Whiteside, "[and it] is a sure-fire way to shorten the life of your glove." Treat leather as you would your own skin. Don't expose your glove to harsh temperatures for any length of time. Certainly don't bake your glove in an oven, or nuke it in the microwave. "This is the worst thing you could do to your glove!" says Whiteside. Heat dries out the leather, and excessive dryness causes the glove's leather to become brittle and deteriorate faster than normal. Whiteside also warns against submerging your glove in water. "This will cause the glove to become heavy."

⑥ Another way to form the pocket (when you can't find a buddy to play catch with) is by pounding and beating on the glove. Throw a ball into the glove as hard and as frequently as you can. You can also pound the pocket with a mallet, hammer, bat, or your fist. This is a cathartic activity when you need to relieve stress. Be sure to pound exactly where you want the pocket to be formed. You can also visit a batting cage, and, if money is no object, instead of hitting the balls, use the machine to help break in the glove by catching the balls.

⑦ In general, regular use is the best way to soften up a baseball glove and form the pocket. "There is no shortcut to breaking in a new glove," says Whiteside. "The best way to form a pocket is to play catch." As you play catch, keep bending and shaping the glove. Over time, the glove will conform to your hand and your style of catching the ball.

 Rawlings Gold Glove Awards for fielding excellence has been presented to a major-league player from each position in each league each season since 1957.

Fielding Grounders

DAVID ECKSTEIN
2006 World Series Most Valuable Player

Always try to field a ground ball while moving toward the ball.

① An infielder should always be ready to field a grounder, so start in an athletic stance. "Keep your knees bent, your shoulders down, and your head set," says Eckstein, the shortstop on two World Series–winning teams: the 2002 Anaheim Angels and the 2006 St. Louis Cardinals. As the pitcher begins the windup, shift your weight onto the balls of your feet so you will be ready to move quickly in either direction.

② Keep your eye on the ball as the pitch is delivered. Extend your glove in front of you with the open pocket facing out. A player in fielding position for a grounder should have the tip of the glove on the ground,

touching the dirt, because if the ball bounces awkwardly, it's easier to go from the ground up to field the ball.

③ A player should always try to field a ground ball while moving toward the ball. "Never back up on a grounder," says Eckstein, "because then the ball plays you, instead of you playing the ball." As a ground ball comes toward you, charge the ball with small, short steps so that you don't run past it. "I'm right-handed, so I step with my right foot first and then my left," says the two-time All-Star.

④ As you near the ball, keep your legs at least shoulder-width apart and your knees bent and head up. Keep your glove out and center yourself so your whole body is behind the ball. When you're picking up the ball, make sure your glove is pointed toward the ground and create a mouth with your throwing hand to secure the grab.

⑤ After fielding the ball, don't get fancy when transferring it from your glove to your throwing hand. Use your free hand to take the ball out of the glove, rather than flipping it out. It's also important to make a good throw to get the base runner out. "When you come up, you should have your shoulders squared to your target," says Eckstein.

David Eckstein has a career .980 fielding percentage. He's made only 98 errors in nearly 1,200 games since 2001.

Shagging Outfield Flies

JACOBY ELLSBURY
Major-League Outfielder

Keep your eye on the ball and your glove out of your face.

① Proper outfield play begins with the ready position. Players should stand facing home plate, with their knees slightly bent and feet square. Weight should be placed on the balls of the feet, and the glove should be at waist level. "This will allow you to move in any direction once the ball is hit," says Ellsbury, center fielder for the 2007 World Series–winning Boston Red Sox.

② Once the ball is in the air, take a moment to judge where it's going so that you don't head in the wrong direction. Ellsbury recommends pausing "because it's easier to go forward on a ball, and it allows you to make a better decision."

③ When a fly ball comes a player's way, he should always try to catch the ball with two hands. "It's one of the most important things an outfielder should do," he says. Your throwing hand can act as a safety net in case the ball doesn't hit your glove cleanly. Also, by catching the ball with two hands you will be able to get the ball out of your glove and make the throw quicker.

④ To catch a fly ball, a player should keep his two thumbs together with the glove pointed up to field it. Keep your eye on the ball and your glove out of your face. The arms should be extended to reach out for the ball, but the player shouldn't stab at it. The glove should be kept wide open to accept the ball, and the other hand should be close by to help guide the ball into the glove. A player's arms should give with the ball as it enters the glove.

⑤ The outfield is no place for daydreaming. Before the batter swings, make sure you're aware of the situation. Always know how many outs there are, how many runners are on base, and where you should throw the ball if it's hit to you. "When it's time to make the catch, position your body so it's facing the target you want to throw to," says Ellsbury, who has made only two errors in three major-league seasons.

⑥ To prepare to throw after a catch, put your throwing hand close to your glove so that it will be easy to grab the ball and throw. Point your non-throwing shoulder at your target. Then follow through by bringing your back leg forward so you can get more leverage—and more velocity—on your throw. "Aim for the bill of the cap [of the player you are throwing to]," says Ellsbury. "If you miss, you're likely to hit him in the middle of the body, so it's still easy for him to catch it."

 Fast Fact

Jacoby Ellsbury led the American League in stolen bases in 2008 and 2009.

Stealing a Base

JUAN PIERRE
Stolen Bases Champion

Getting a good jump is the key to being a successful base stealer.

① Get a strong lead. The length of your lead away from the base should be approximately one body length plus a foot. This will allow you to get back to the base easily if the pitcher tries to pick you off. "But as a base stealer, you can't be afraid to get picked off," say Pierre, the National League stolen bases champion in 2001 and 2003.

② As you are leading, your weight should be on the balls of your feet and your knees should be bent. Focus on the pitcher to determine when to start running. If a right-handed pitcher lifts his left foot first, he's throwing home. If he lifts his right, he's throwing to first. "With a right-handed pitcher, I'm keying on the heel of his left foot," says Pierre, who has stolen 459 bases since the 2000 season.

③ Getting a good jump is the key to being a successful base stealer. Begin with a small step with your lead foot. You want to get it up and put it down quickly and use your crossover step.

④ Once you get a jump, try to accelerate and stay as low as possible. Gradually come up, like a sprinter. Once you are in full stride, focus on the base and sprint as fast as you can toward it.

⑤ As you run, concentrate on the base. Pay attention to where the fielder's feet are set up, and try to maneuver to the inside or outside the bag to avoid them. Slide to the back side of the base. It is recommended that base runners slide feetfirst.

⑥ Start your slide about 5 feet away from the base. Stick one leg straight out and tuck the other leg under your thigh. Keep your hands up and your back off the dirt. "If you can see where the ball is heading, try to slide around the tag," says Pierre, a member of the 2003 World Series–winning Florida Marlins.

⑦   When you slide, accelerate into the bag. Don't slide past the base. Says Pierre: "The number-one key is to stay on the bag."

Juan Pierre is the fourth player in MLB history to successfully swipe 100 or more bases for three different teams: the Florida Marlins, Colorado Rockies, and Los Angeles Dodgers. (The other players are Otis Nixon, Brett Butler, and Tommy Harper.)

Firing a Fastball

JASON MARQUIS
All-Star Pitcher

Quick Tip

Generate power from your legs, not your arm.

① Stand upright on the pitching rubber, hide the ball in your glove, and focus your eyes on the catcher's target. "The main thing is to keep your body under control," says Marquis, a 2009 All-Star for the Colorado Rockies. "You want to be balanced over the pitching rubber as you begin your windup."

② Use the windup to gain power. As you begin, lift your hands and raise the knee opposite your pitching arm. Marquis is a righty, so before transferring his weight forward, he comes to his "balance point" by balancing on the ball of his right foot. He steps toward home plate with his left leg.

③ To maintain his balance, Marquis lands on the ball of his left foot, with the foot pointed toward home. "As you make your delivery, you want to have all your momentum going toward home plate while still staying balanced." To generate power, "you want to release the ball [when] your entire body is moving forward." Marquis releases the ball with his elbow shoulder-high and his weight going forward. This motion allows him to channel all the energy he has generated into the pitch. "Don't squeeze the ball too tightly, and don't try to throw too hard. Your power should come from your legs, not your arm."

④ The four-seam fastball is the classic fastball grip. Hold the ball across the wide, horseshoe-shaped seam with your middle and index fingers spread a half inch apart. Your thumb supports the underside of the ball. With this grip, expect the pitch to rise as it makes its way to the catcher. "The index finger and the middle finger are across the seams," says

Marquis. As the ball comes out of your hand, you are naturally forcing it to rotate. (The ball sliding off your fingertips causes backspin.) The faster you can get the ball to rotate, the more power you can generate on the pitch. To increase the rotation of the pitch, snap your wrist slightly as you release the ball.

⑤ To throw a two-seam fastball, grip the ball with your index and middle fingers across two seams, at the point where the laces are closest to each other. Squeeze the ball with the tips of your fingers and the side of your thumb. The two-seamer's sinking motion makes it great for getting groundballs. "Your finger pressure is coming off two laces [instead of four]," says Marquis, who has ninety-four career victories with four teams since entering the major leagues in 2000. "A lot of people call it a sinker. I'm right-handed, so for me the ball will move from left to right. It will have some downward sink to it because of the finger pressure and the way the laces are coming out of my hand."

⑥ After releasing the pitch, continue the motion of your arm and follow through with your body. Allow your natural momentum to carry your body forward. Be sure to end in a fielding position in case the batter hits a ball back at you. "Once you've released the pitch you become [another] infielder," says Marquis.

 Fast Fact Jason Marquis pitched a no-hitter for Staten Island (N.Y.) in the Little League World Series in 1991, and is one of the few players to participate in the Little League World Series and Major League Baseball World Series (2006 St. Louis Cardinals).

Making a Knuckleball Dance

TIM WAKEFIELD
All-Star Knuckleball Pitcher

Quick Tip   Throw the ball with as little spin as possible.

① Tim Wakefield wants to clear up a misunderstanding. He doesn't throw a knuckleball using his knuckles. "It's my fingernails digging into the ball," says the winner of 189 career games since his major-league debut in 1992. His fingernails are strong and well cared for. "Knuckleball pitchers give themselves manicures all the time." (Indeed, an emery board fell from the back pocket of knuckleball pitcher Joe Niekro's uniform pants while he was standing on the mound during a game in 1987.)

② The knuckleball pitcher's intent is to throw the ball with as little spin or rotation as possible, causing the ball to dart suddenly in one

direction and then veer unexpectedly in another. The knuckleball is a pitch that takes time and practice to master. "Every knuckleball pitcher has a slightly different grip," says Wakefield, a member of the 2004 and 2007 World Series–winning Boston Red Sox teams. "Experiment [throwing the pitch] until you find a grip that's comfortable for you."

③ A common way to grip a knuckleball is by pressing the fingernails of your index, middle, and ring fingers into the ball just below the seams. Keep your thumb underneath the ball as it rests gently against your palm for support, and let your pinkie dangle. A right-handed pitcher, Wakefield uses a two-finger grip, with his right pinky hanging loosely off the ball, as if holding a fancy china teacup.

④ Don't shot put the ball. Throw a knuckleball using your usual fastball motion; just don't snap your wrist when you throw the pitch. As you release the ball, extend your fingers straight out toward home plate. "Think of it more like flicking the ball [out of your hand]," says Wakefield. Make sure you throw the pitch with maximum velocity for maximum movement.

⑤ A knuckleball pitcher should be mentally tough, says Wakefield, because throwing the pitch leaves little margin for error. Make a mistake by putting too much spin on the ball, and it may be hit "475 feet in the opposite direction," he says. "Fastball pitchers can get away with mistakes at 95 [miles per hour], but a poorly thrown knuckleball never works."

Tim Wakefield was a first-time All-Star in 2009, at age forty-two.

Framing a Pitch

JASON KENDALL
All-Star Catcher

Catch the ball in the webbing of your glove.

(1) Crouch down with your knees facing the pitcher. Position yourself about 2 feet behind home plate. "Get close to the batter, but not so close that you get hit by a swing," says Kendall, a three-time All-Star catcher with the Pittsburgh Pirates in 1996, 1998, and 2000.

(2) While in the crouching position, use your glove to give the pitcher an inviting target. Open the glove wide at the spot where the pitch is to be thrown.

③ Shift your body weight onto the balls of your feet to be as mobile as possible. "If no runners are on base, you can sit in a more relaxed position," says Kendall, who has caught 1,907 career games with four different teams since 1996. Keep your throwing hand in a fist behind the glove. The fist will protect your fingers.

④ Catch the ball in the webbing of your glove. "Frame" the pitch for the umpire by seamlessly moving the glove toward the middle of your body and behind home plate as soon as the ball hits your glove.

⑤ Unless a runner is stealing or the pitch is hit, stay in your crouch to avoid blocking the umpire's view of the pitch. Says Kendall: "On a close pitch, the umpire might be swayed to call a strike."

Jason Kendall is a second-generation major-league catcher; his father, Fred, was a backstop from 1969 to 1980.

Keeping Score at a Ball Game

BILL SHANNON
Official Scorer for Major League Baseball

When scoring for souvenir purposes, keep it simple.

① Buy a program or scorecard from a vendor at the game. Most all supply a pencil. Jot down the lineups. "Modern score sheets commonly include printed grids and diagrams," says Shannon. The spaces on the left side of the grid are for players' names, positions, and uniform numbers. Numbers on the top of the grid are the innings. The bottom spaces indicate the totals of each team's hits and runs scored.

② A list of abbreviations in each player's box represents the ways to reach base safely: single (1B), double (2B), triple (3B), home run (HR), walk (BB—for base on balls), and hit by pitch (HBP).

③ In the simplest system, the scorer follows each batter around the diamond on the score sheet, starting at home plate. When a runner reaches base, draw a line to that base and indicate how he reached that base by drawing a line through the appropriate abbreviation. Then continue the line to each base on the diamond the runner subsequently reaches. Indicate a stolen base as SB (placed at the corner of the base stolen) and a sacrifice hit as SH.

④ A completed line around the diamond represents a run scored. An uncompleted diamond shows that the runner has been left on base and indicates which base he reached before the third out ended the inning. Says Shannon: "Fill in the diamond to easily count the runs scored."

⑤ Fielders are numbered by position. Pitcher (1), catcher (2), first baseman (3), second baseman (4), third baseman (5), shortstop (6), left fielder (7), center fielder (8), and right fielder (9). Batters' outs are indicated by using the number of each fielder handling the ball. "When

scoring for souvenir purposes, keep it simple," says Shannon. For example, a fly out to right field is marked as F9. A line drive caught by the center fielder is indicated as L8. A pop-up to second base is P4. Use K for a strikeout.

⑥ Score ground outs by marking the numbers of the players making the throw and the catch. If the batter hits a ground ball to the third baseman and is thrown out at first, write 5-3, or 5-4 if the third baseman throws to second base for the force out. Mark the numbers of all the fielders involved in a double play. For example, mark 6-4-3 to note a double play started by the shortstop. When a fielder takes a ground ball and makes the out unassisted, such as a first baseman stepping on the bag, the play is indicated as 3U. "Keep track of each out by writing the number of the out in the lower left-hand corner of the box, and draw a circle around it," says Shannon.

⑦ Errors are shown as E6 for an error by the shortstop or E7 for an error by the left fielder. A wild pitch is indicated by WP and a passed ball as PB. The five small squares in the lower right section of each box are provided for the scorer to keep track of the balls and strikes count on the batter.

⑧ Says Shannon: "Over time, most scorers will develop their own personal system." Whatever your method, the result should be a complete record of every player in every inning and a shorthand explanation of how the game played out.

Bill Shannon has served as one of New York's official scorers for Mets and Yankees home games since 1979.

Snagging a Souvenir Ball

ZACK HAMPLE

Author, *How to Snag Major League Baseballs*

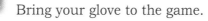

Bring your glove to the game.

① Most baseball fans go to a major-league game hoping to catch a ball that is hit into the stands. A baseball makes a great souvenir, yet most fans believe the odds are against them. "It's not as hard as it seems," says Hample. "And players love to throw balls to kids." Here's how you can walk away from the ballpark with a souvenir baseball in your pocket.

② Make sure to bring your glove to the game. When a foul ball is coming at you at 90 miles per hour, you're going to want to protect yourself. Also, most balls popped foul are twisting and spinning coming off the bat. Catching a ball with so much spin bare-handed is nearly impossible. So put your glove on.

③ Teams begin warming up on the field about two hours before game time, so arrive at the ballpark early, when fewer people are competing against you. When teams are warming up, they often toss balls to their fans in the stands. "'Please' goes a long way," says Hample, who can say "Please throw me a ball" in several different languages, and once even used sign language with a deaf player.

④ If you get near a player who has a ball in his hand, politely ask him for it. "Don't call [the player] 'Yo!' or "Hey, you!' and don't make annoying whistling noises. Always use [the player's] first name. Last names are phony and overly formal. Be loud and always say please."

⑤ Go to batting practice. This is your best chance to snag a baseball. "There are fewer fans, and security isn't as strict," says Hample. Most batters are right-handed and will pull the ball during batting practice. By placing yourself in left field, you up your chances of snagging a ball. And make sure you stand on the aisle. "Don't get trapped in the middle of a long row. You need to be able to jump up and move," he says.

⑥ Buy a cap for each team that's playing, and change your cap according to which team is on the field. Players on the road love to spot their fans, and will often reward them by throwing them a ball. "Visiting teams love to reward their fans, so wear the opponents' gear," says Hample. "Just prepare to be heckled."

⑦ Snagging a ball during the game is much more difficult than during pre-game drills. The ideal place to be is on the aisle next to the field, about three quarters of the way from third base to the foul pole. It's easy to reach over and field ground foul balls—but only if the wall separating the stands from the field is low enough to reach over. "It's important to know the stadium, so do your research," says Hample. If the walls are high, your chances might be better if you go a little farther back to catch a foul pop-up.

⑧ With ground balls that roll near the wall, make sure it's a foul ball before you reach over and grab it. If you touch a ball in play or reach out onto the field and interfere with a live ball, you will likely be ejected from the stadium. "Don't get in the way of the players," says Hample.

⑨ Snagging a ball during the game takes more strategy than trying to snag one during batting practice, so plan ahead and play the percentages. Check out the pitching matchups ahead of time so you know how many right- and left-handed batters are likely to be in the starting lineup. Most right-handed batters will hit foul balls to the first-base side; left-handed batters to the third-base side. According to Hample, 99 percent of foul balls are sliced the opposite way, so select a seat in the stadium accordingly. "For a right-hander, I draw an imaginary line from the left fielder through home plate," says Hample. "That's the perfect place to sit."

 Zack Hample has snagged more than 4,300 baseballs at forty-six different major-league stadiums across North America since 1990.

Spitting Sunflower Seeds like a Major Leaguer

ORLANDO HUDSON
Two-time All-Star

Eat the seed. Spit the shell.

① Get a bag of sunflower seeds with the seeds still in their shells. Pour a handful of seeds into the palm of your hand. Remove any seeds with broken shells and seeds with stems.

② Put about five seeds into your mouth and use your tongue to push them into your right cheek. "Pack the seeds like a beaver uses his tail to pack the wood and mud together to build a dam," says Hudson, an

All-Star with the Arizona Diamondbacks in 2007 and the Los Angeles Dodgers in 2009.

③ Use your tongue to shift one seed over to the left side of your mouth. Crack the shell of the seed using your left-side teeth.

④ Now move the shell away from the seed using your tongue. Chew and swallow the seed.

⑤ Get the shell to stick to the tip of your tongue and move it to the front of your mouth. Then spit out the shell. But be careful not to hit your teammates with it. "That's nasty," says Hudson.

 Orlando Hudson has won four Gold Glove awards for fielding excellence at second base.

Basketball

Swishing More Foul Shots

GRANT HILL

Seven-time NBA All-Star

 Aim for a target at the back of the rim.

① Maintaining good balance is the key to successful foul shooting. Position your feet shoulder-width apart, parallel and pointing toward the basket. Square your upper body to the basket, too. Stand just behind the free-throw line.

② Use your nonshooting hand to gently cradle the ball. Place the middle three fingers of your shooting hand on the seams of the ball, with your thumb and palm acting as support. "Rest the ball on the fingertips of your shooting hand," says Hill, a 76.4 percent career free-throw shooter. "Keep your other hand on the side of the ball and use it as a guide."

③ Aim for a target at the back of the rim, so you won't shoot the ball short. A good target is the shooting square drawn on the backboard above the rim.

④ Don't jump when taking a foul shot. Bend your knees, and in one fluid shooting motion, propel the shot upward by straightening your knees. "Push off with your legs," says Hill, "but stay grounded."

⑤ When you release the ball, keep your shooting arm straight toward the basket, not tilted to one side. "To shoot, extend your arm," says the 1995 NBA co-Rookie of the Year. "Keep your elbows close to your body."

⑥ Release the ball with your fingertips. "Follow through by snapping your shooting wrist down, for good backspin," says Hill. Backspin allows for better control of the shot and a softer arc off the rim.

⑦ Practice your foul shooting and develop a routine. Most players bounce the ball or spin it in their hands before setting up for their free throws. Every time you practice a foul shot, use the routine. "Every player needs a routine that works for them," says Hill.

⑧ Take your time at the line and concentrate on good shot fundamentals. This is the only time in the game when a player can focus on proper execution of the shooting technique without worrying about the defense. "They're called *free* throws for a reason," says Hill. "They're free points, and nobody's guarding you."

Grant Hill's father, Calvin, was a three-time NFL All-Pro running back with the Dallas Cowboys in the 1970s.

Shooting a Pull-up Jumper

DAVID WEST
Two-time NBA All-Star

 Take a step back to create space between you and the defender.

① If you're having trouble beating your opponent to the basket, try a pull-up jumper. Start to drive to the basket as if you're going in for a layup.

② Stop your drive and let the defender's momentum carry him toward the basket. Take a step back as you stop dribbling to create space between you and the defender.

③ As you step back, square your feet and shoulders to the basket. This puts you in the best position to take a jump shot. "Keep your head forward," says West, who was the eighteenth overall selection by the New Orleans Hornets in the 2003 NBA Draft. "A lot of players start to tilt their head back, and they lose their balance and shoot a fadeaway jumper."

④ To shoot a jump shot, jump straight into the air. Keep your legs and back straight while you are in the air. Release the ball when you are at the highest point of your jump. That makes it more difficult for the defender to block your shot. Land on the same spot from which you jumped.

⑤ Keep the elbow of your shooting arm tucked in close to your body, and keep your elbow under the ball. That keeps your body in line and your form intact. If your arms are too wide, you'll have trouble being consistent with your shot.

⑥ Don't forget to follow through with your wrist bent forward toward the basket. "Always put backspin on the ball when you release

it," says West, who scored an average of 21 points per game during the 2008–09 season. It is easier to spin the ball if you spread your fingers wide and hold the ball with your fingertips, not on the palm of your hand.

David West was the 2003 College Player of the Year while attending Xavier University.

Improving Your 3-Point Shot

STEVE KERR
NBA Record Holder

 Your aim shouldn't change when you are shooting a trey.

① Before you begin practicing 3-pointers, it's important to have good form on your basic jump shot. "You have to have proper balance, with your feet at least shoulder-width apart and a deep knee bend that is going to [help] you get the ball to the rim," says Kerr, whose career 45.4 percent, 3-point field-goal percentage is the best in NBA history.

② When you're ready to step behind the arc, realize that much of your power is going to come from your legs, not the arms or shoulders. "The farther you are away from the basket, the more your lower body is going to come into play," says Kerr, winner of the 1997 All-Star Game 3-Point Shootout.

③ The same shooting form is always used regardless of how far the player is from the basket. The only difference between a jump shot from 10 feet or 20 feet is more leg power is required in the jump for the longer shot.

④ Try to hold the ball the same way every time you shoot, "so that you have the same backspin on your shot consistently." The ball should be centered in the palm of your shooting hand. It's also important that you follow through with your wrist bent forward toward the basket.

⑤ Although most NBA players release the ball above their shoulder, "the release point for kids is going to be lower, somewhere around your upper chest," says Kerr. To generate the most power, release the ball just before the top of your jump.

⑥ Don't change where you aim your shot when you are shooting a trey. "If you aim at the front of the rim, the back of the rim, or the entire basket, it shouldn't change if you're shooting a 6-foot shot, a 16-foot shot, or a 3-point shot," says Kerr, currently the team president of the Phoenix Suns.

⑦ Give your shot some arc. A common problem poor shooters share is the lack of arc. A ball shot with arc is more likely to go into the hoop than a shot with the arc of a line drive.

⑧ Don't get bummed when you miss a shot. Just keep shooting. "You have to have confidence that the shot will go in," says Kerr. "Sometimes it doesn't, but keep shooting. If you miss, you can always blame the rim!"

Steve Kerr played on five NBA Championship teams as a member of the Chicago Bulls and San Antonio Spurs.

Shooting a Turnaround Jumper

SWIN CASH
Three-time WNBA All-Star

Fade away as you shoot to create separation between you and your defender.

① Position yourself on the right or left side of the block, 2 feet above the baseline. Don't set up too far away from the basket—no more than 10 feet out. Know your shooting range and stay within it.

② Create a good target to receive the pass. Maintain balance by keeping your feet shoulder-width apart, with knees slightly bent and your backside low. Know where your defender is before you shoot. This will help you avoid getting your shot blocked. "I always look over both shoulders first," says Cash, the 2009 WNBA All-Star Game Most Valuable Player.

③ When shooting the turnaround jumper, you can turn to either side. Cash, a right-handed shooter, prefers to turn to her right. The shorter turn makes it easier for her to square her body to the basket when she shoots. Reverse the directions if you are left-handed.

④ Try to fake your defender by turning your shoulders and head slightly to the left. When the defender reacts to the fake, then pivot off your right foot *away* from the basket.

⑤ As you pivot, swing your left leg around. Your body will shield the ball from the defender. Continue to pivot until your body faces the basket. "If you keep the ball above your shoulders after catching the pass you will get the shot off faster," says Cash, a member of the 2003 WNBA Champion Detroit Shock.

⑥ When you are square to the basket, raise your arms in a shooting position. Your form should be the same as for a regular jump shot. Keep

your guide hand on the ball. Your shooting elbow should be in an L shape. The ball should be set slightly above your head. "[This] makes it tough for the defender to block your shot," says Cash, currently a member of the Seattle Storm.

⑦ Begin to jump, and get ready to release the ball. Fade away slightly as you shoot to create more space between you and your opponent. "Create separation between you and your defender."

⑧ Release the ball at the peak of your jump. The shot should have enough arc to get over the rim. Flick the wrist of your shooting hand down on the follow-through to create backspin.

⑨ Practice the move and focus on the shooting technique—the catch, pivot, and jump shot all in one smooth movement—while maintaining good balance.

Swin Cash played with the 2000 and 2002 NCAA Champion Connecticut Huskies and was a member of the 2004 U.S. Olympic gold medal–winning squad.

Dribbling like a Point Guard

CHRIS DUHON
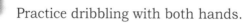
NBA Point Guard

Quick Tip

Practice dribbling with both hands.

① Bounce the ball off your fingertips, not the palm of your hand. As you bounce the ball, keep it close to your body and slightly to your side.

② Keep your dribbling hand at waist level. If you dribble the ball too high, another player might steal it from you.

③ Keep your head up and look in front of you as you dribble. Duhon suggests setting up obstacles like chairs and cones to dribble around. "You

want to make sure you can handle defensive pressure," he says. "You don't want anyone to strip the ball away from you."

④ Learn to play with both hands. All players should be able to control the ball with either hand. "Try dribbling with one hand behind your back," says Duhon, point guard for the 2001 NCAA Champion Duke Blue Devils.

⑤ While at practice, don't just work on your shooting. Focus on your dribbling, too. Duhon recommends dribbling to the free-throw line from the baseline, then back to the baseline. Next go to half-court and back. Finally, dribble the length of the court and back. "Try to change speeds every time you change directions," says Duhon. The variation will improve your ballhandling in game situations.

Chris Duhon set the New York Knicks' single-game franchise record with 22 assists on November 29, 2008.

Learning the Crossover Dribble

DERRICK ROSE
2009 NBA Rookie of the Year

Your feet are an important part of the crossover dribble.

① Once you have mastered the dribbling fundamentals (see Dribbling like a Point Guard) you are ready to attempt a crossover dribble. In this maneuver, a player switches the ball rapidly from one hand to the other, enabling him or her to quickly change direction, shake free from an opponent, and drive to the hoop.

② The crossover move is most effective when the player is able to convince the defense that he intends to dribble in one direction, and then bursts past them in the other direction while switching the ball to the opposite hand.

③ The crossover dribble needs to be a low, quick bounce. The ball will be vulnerable when it crosses in front of the defensive player, so keep an arm's length between you and the defender. "It's important to have room to pull a crossover, so give yourself space" says Rose, the number-one overall pick by the Chicago Bulls in the 2008 NBA Draft. "You don't want the [opponent] to be too close, otherwise he can reach his hand in and strip the ball from you."

④ Be aware of your feet. Even though you dribble with your hands, your feet are still an important part of the crossover. "The coach who taught me to crossover taught me how to shift my weight," says Rose. "If you want to do a quick crossover from left to right, push off your right and then your left foot."

⑤ Once the player jabs hard in the direction of the fake, he needs to push off hard in the opposite direction. "It's the first step off the jab that

will either get you past the defense or not," says Rose. The foot that is jabbing in the direction of the fake must plant firm; this is the push-off foot for the explosive dribble past the defender to follow the fake.

⑥ Always be thinking forward. The fastest crossover in the world is useless if it doesn't help get you any closer to the basket. "A lot of people crossover but don't cover any ground moving forward," says Rose, who averaged 16.8 points per game with 6.3 assists to lead all rookies during the 2008–09 season. "You want to be going to the hoop."

Derrick Rose scored 36 points in his first post-season game to equal Kareem Abdul-Jabbar's record for most points scored by a rookie making his NBA play-off debut.

Dribbling Drill

A player needs manual dexterity to maintain ball control to perform the crossover dribble without letting the ball slip out of his hands. Here's a good drill to strengthen your dribbling skills.

Practice dribbling by standing with knees bent and feet shoulder-width apart. Move the ball between your legs in a figure-eight motion. Don't lose control of the ball. When you feel comfortable, go a little faster. Then try *dribbling* the ball between your legs in the figure-eight motion.

Making a Perfect Bounce Pass

STEVE BLAKE
NBA Point Guard

Aim for a spot three quarters of the way between you and your teammate.

① Always pass the ball with two hands. Hold the ball at waist level with both thumbs behind the ball.

② To gain velocity on your bounce pass, push the ball away from your body by extending your arms in a quick, downward motion. "Make sure you get equal power from both arms," says Blake, who tied the NBA record with 14 assists in one quarter on February 22, 2009. "Two arms are stronger than one."

③ When you make a bounce pass, the ball should come off your fingertips, not your palms. Follow through by snapping your wrists. On release, your thumbs push through the ball and your palms face outward.

④ When your teammate is on the move, a bounce pass is easier to handle than a chest pass or overhead pass. Aim for a spot three quarters of the way between you and your teammate. Try to bounce the ball off this spot.

⑤ Step into the pass. Push off your back foot and take a step forward with your front foot. Lead the ball far enough in front so your teammate can catch the ball in stride. "The bounce pass is difficult for a defender to steal, because [the ball] changes direction," says the Portland Trail Blazers' point guard.

⑥ Practice the trajectory and speed of your bounce pass to increase accuracy. Learn to fake and use misdirection so as not to telegraph your pass. "A pass moves the ball up the court faster than a player dribbling on the run," says Blake. "So if you see an open teammate, pass him the rock."

 Steve Blake was a member of the 2002 NCAA Champion Maryland Terrapins.

Boxing Out for a Rebound

HERB BROWN
NBA Assistant Coach

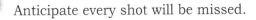 Anticipate every shot will be missed.

① Size has relatively little to do with rebounding ability. "Size is helpful, but it isn't the most important factor to being a good rebounder," says Brown, currently an assistant coach with the Charlotte Bobcats. The more essential skills are positioning and boxing out.

② A smaller player who can effectively box out will hold his own against bigger opponents. The right attitude is also imperative. "Be relentless in going after the ball," says Brown, previously an assistant coach with the 2004 NBA Champion Detroit Pistons. "Anticipate every shot will be a miss."

③ When a shot goes up, don't immediately turn to the basket and wait for the rebound to come to you. "That's a big mistake," says Brown. "A smart opponent will get around you and grab [the ball]." Instead, wait a moment after the shot is released to see if your opponent is trying to gain position by going around you to the left or right. Once the offensive player commits to a direction, the defender can pivot that way and box out.

④ The objective of boxing out your opponent is not to gain position. "If you play good defense, you should already have position; you should already be between the offensive player and the basket," says Brown. The objective of boxing out is to momentarily freeze your opponent so that the opponent can't get to the rebound. "Otherwise, he'll just go around you and snatch the ball away."

⑤ To freeze the offensive player, the defender is going to pivot into him and seal off the lane to the basket. Make solid contact, with your butt sitting squarely on the offensive player's thigh. "The contact has to be on the [offensive player's] thigh, because that will stop [your opponent] from jumping," says Brown. The defender needs to be in a low defensive stance to stay balanced and to move quickly for the ball.

⑥ When a shot is taken, watch the arc of the ball as it travels in the air toward the basket. Most of the time, the ball will bounce back in the same direction from which it was shot, and land about two-thirds of the distance back to the shooter. "The longer the shot, the longer the rebound," says Brown. "Be aggressive and protect the ball once you get it."

⑦ Even if you box out a bigger opponent, it's still too easy for him to reach over you and grab the ball. Brown suggests another way to help your team rebound. When a shot goes up, turn and face your opponent. With your arms crossed, use your body to push him away from the basket. Make sure you don't use your arms to push off, or you might get whistled for a foul. Pushing the opponent out of the way clears the lane for one of your teammates to get the rebound. "Ideally, all five defensive players are rebounders," says Brown.

 Herb Brown was named Coach of the Year in the Western Basketball Association and the Continental Basketball Association and college Coach of the Year with Stony Brook in 1969.

Fronting the Post

HERB BROWN
NBA Assistant Coach

A defender should always have his body between the basket and the player he is guarding.

① If your opponent hasn't reached the post yet, beat him to the spot and stay in front of him. Your knees should be bent and you should be in a defensive stance with your hands up. Try to keep your opponent from establishing position down low. "If your opponent gets the ball down low, he's in control," says Brown, head coach of the Detroit Pistons during the 1975–76 NBA season.

② As your opponent establishes position, crouch down in your defensive stance. "If you get low on an opponent's hips you can control the way he moves," says Brown. Maintain contact with the player you are guarding to gain leverage and also to feel where the opponent is at all times.

③ Post players need to deny the pass in from the wing. The idea is to have a hand in the passing lane so that the passer doesn't see a clear path or, if he does try to make the pass, the defender can swat it away.

"Fronting the post is not effective unless the defense is putting pressure on the ball," say Brown, an assistant coach with six different NBA teams, including the Philadelphia 76ers team that reached the 2001 finals.

④ Proper denial position means the defender must straddle the offensive player by placing one foot on the side of the offensive player, slightly to the rear, and the other foot slightly in front, with the front arm stretched out ahead of the offensive player in the area where he would receive the ball. "Always have a hand in the passing lane," says Brown. "Slap the ball away using your hand [that is] nearest the ball." The hand in back should be touching the offensive player so you can feel every move made by your opponent.

⑤ A shut-down defender will always have his body between the basket and the opposing player. The defender should rely on peripheral vision to watch the player he is guarding and the offensive team's ball movement simultaneously, and to quickly adjust position when necessary. "When the ball moves, you move with the ball to maintain the front," says Brown.

⑥ Brown recommends using your forearms to push against your opponent "and root him out of position." If your opponent receives the ball on the block, continue to lean against him with your body. "Be careful not to lean on one side of his body more than the other," says Brown. "Otherwise, he'll know which way he can spin off you." Pushing your opponent away from the basket forces the player to settle for an outside shot, rather than drive for an easy layup. When the player takes a jump shot, put a hand in your opponent's face to contest the shot.

Spinning a Basketball on Your Finger

MICHAEL "WILD THING" WILSON
Harlem Globetrotters

Practice. A lot.

(1) Use a basketball that is sized for young players. Hold the ball with the fingertips of both hands in front of your body about chest-high, with the seams running from top to bottom.

(2) Toss the ball into the air and, at the same time, spin it away from you. "Throw it about face level," says Wilson, a member of the Harlem Globetrotters from 1996 to 2006.

③ Try to catch the ball with the tip of your index finger at the spot on the ball where the seams meet. There's a smooth groove there that makes it easier to control the ball. "You know when the teacher tells you the earth rotates on its axis?" asks Wilson, who played collegiate ball at Memphis from 1994 to 1996. "Your finger is like the axis. And the ball represents the earth."

④ Gently tap the ball with your other hand to keep it spinning. "You need a lot of practice to master the skill," says Wilson.

Michael "Wild Thing" Wilson set a world record with a 12-foot dunk in 2000.

Football

Dropping Back like a Pro Quarterback

MATT RYAN
2008 NFL Rookie of the Year

Keep the football under your chin and both hands on the ball.

① The three-step drop-back is the basic footwork for a high-percentage short pass from the pocket. In a three-step drop-back, routes are quick to develop, so it's critical that the quarterback deliver the ball to the receiver in stride. "You want the receiver to [gain] yards after the catch," says Ryan, the third pick in the 2008 NFL Draft by the Atlanta Falcons.

② After receiving the snap from center, take a big step back with the foot on the same side as your passing hand. (Right-handers step back with their right foot. If you are left-handed, use your left foot in these directions.) "Make sure you clear the feet of the offensive linemen so you don't get tripped up," says Ryan. As you take your first step back, turn your body to face the sideline.

③ Take your second step by crossing your left foot over your right foot, staying on a straight line. "Don't take a sack by drifting left or right [into a defensive lineman]," Ryan cautions. Take your third step with your right foot, balancing your weight as you land. "Your upper body should be leaning slightly toward the target," says Ryan. Plant your right foot on the last step, take a step toward your target with your left foot, and throw.

④ A three-step drop should take the passer 5 yards deep, which gives enough space to throw without hitting your hand on an offensive lineman's helmet. When you practice your three-step drop, Ryan suggests counting in your head as you take your drop. "Think 1-2-3-balance and throw," he says. "And make sure you get your depth."

⑤ For the five-step drop, the quarterback will be adding an additional two steps from the three-step drop. Your fourth step should be shorter, with your left foot crossing your right again. Your fifth step, with your right foot, is also short. On the final step, the quarterback must plant with the back foot and shuffle forward slightly to get a little closer to the line of scrimmage. "Shuffle forward to gain momentum but still stay in the pocket [created by the offensive linemen] when you deliver the ball," says Ryan, whose first professional pass went for a 62-yard touchdown play.

⑥ On most five-step drops, the quarterback will be 7 yards deep. Pass patterns requiring a five-step drop take more time to develop, so the quarterback will need to wait for the receiver to finish the route. Don't become flat-footed. "Keep your feet moving," says Ryan. This allows the quarterback to quickly step left or right and throw to either side of the field.

⑦ Finally, while dropping back to pass, Ryan says to "keep the football up under your chin and both hands on the ball." This not only protects the football but also makes you look like a real quarterback!

Matt Ryan is the first rookie quarterback in NFL history to start all sixteen regular-season games and take his team to the playoffs.

Completing More Passes

Quick Tip

You want to be able to look over your front shoulder on a straight line at the receiver.

① Quarterbacks should never stare at the ground while dropping back to pass. "That's a bad habit," says Ryan, who set a NFL rookie single-game playoff record with 26 completions. "Always look downfield so you can recognize the [defensive] coverage and find [the open] receiver."

② When you drop back and plant your back foot, angle your body and point your front foot toward the side of the field you are throwing to. This will prevent you from losing momentum, and, since you're already in a ready position to throw, give you a quicker release.

③ When passing to the throwing-arm side of the field, don't open up your front shoulder too quickly. This will result in your body being too far out ahead of your arm during the throwing motion.

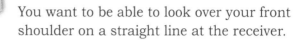

④ When passing to the non-throwing-arm side of the field, inexperienced quarterbacks have a tendency of not stepping toward the target receiver. Staying closed is a big mistake, too, says Ryan, because "then you'll throw [the football] across your body, and that's usually an interception waiting to happen."

⑤ If the quarterback is flushed out of the pocket he must throw on the run. For a right-handed quarterback, throwing on the run to the left is difficult. For lefties, throwing to the right is just as tough. That's why it's important to get your momentum going downfield before you throw.

⑥ As you prepare to throw, square your shoulders and hips toward your target. Says Ryan: "You can't always [twist] all the way around [toward the target], but a big key is to get as far around as you can."

⑦ Push off your right leg and step toward your target with your left foot as you throw. "Make your last step or two toward your target," says Ryan.

 Matt Ryan won the 2009 ESPY Award as the Best Breakthrough Athlete.

Throwing a Perfect Spiral

AARON RODGERS
NFL Quarterback

Flick your throwing hand as you let go of the ball.

① Hold the football in your throwing hand. Place your index finger near the nose of the ball, your middle finger on top of the laces, and your ring and pinky fingers near the middle of the laces. Your non-throwing hand should hold the back of the ball for support, and your feet should be a little more than shoulder-width apart.

② Take a 6-inch step forward as you start to throw. "Avoid taking too big a stride," says Rodgers, who threw for 4,038 yards and 28 touchdowns

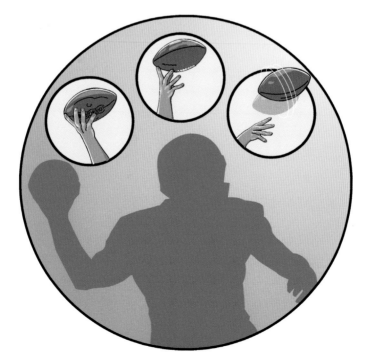

for the Green Bay Packers in 2008. Bring your throwing arm straight up. (Don't wind up.) Your throwing elbow should be a little higher than your shoulder, so your arm "almost makes a backward L shape, with the bottom of the L slanted down."

③ The key to the spiral is the release. Flick your throwing hand as you let go of the ball and follow through by bringing your arm across your body. "The way I think about it is, put your throwing thumb in your opposite pocket," says the Packers' first round selection in the 2005 NFL Draft. "That naturally flicks your hand down. The last thing the ball should come off is your pointer finger." Rodgers adds that one of the biggest mistakes you can make is throwing with all arm. "Use the whole upper torso," he says. "That helps you get a better spiral, and helps your arm last longer because you're not [hurting] your shoulder."

Aaron Rodgers had a streak of 157 consecutive pass attempts without an interception come to an end during the 2008 season.

Faking a Hand Off with Play Action

SAGE ROSENFELS
NFL Quarterback

Exaggerate the hand off by fully extending your arm so that the defense can see the ball.

① Having a strong grip on the ball will help for a successful play-action fake. Hold the ball tight, so that when you extend it for the fake, a defensive player can't knock it from your hand. "Ball security is the first priority," says Rosenfels, who has thrown thirty career touchdown passes with four different teams since 2001. "As soon as you control the ball, pull it into your belly, and get a good handle on it before you make the fake."

②   Convince the opposition that you are running the ball. "Make the play look more like a run than you normally would," says Rosenfels, currently a backup with the Minnesota Vikings. He recommends exaggerating the handoff by fully extending your arm so that the defense can see the ball.

③   Now that you've fooled the defenders, get in position to make a quick, accurate throw. "Settle your feet," says Rosenfels, who tied an NFL single-game record with four fourth-quarter touchdown passes in 2007. Once you've planted, look for your open receiver and release the ball quickly.

 Sage Rosenfels had a 6–4 record as starting quarterback for the Houston Texans during the 2006 through 2008 seasons.

Catching More Touchdowns

TORRY HOLT

Seven-time Pro Bowl Wide Receiver

Your arms should give with the ball as you squeeze it tight to your body.

① Whenever possible, turn your body square to face the football as it's coming at you. Watch the ball all the way into your hands. "You can't run with the ball if you don't catch it first," says Holt, who has seventy-four career touchdown catches.

② To catch a ball above waist level, form a triangle with your hands, palms out, placing the tips of your thumbs together, the tips of your index fingers together, and your other fingers extended. Bend your elbows.

③ If the football is thrown below waist level, form a triangle, palms up, with the tips of your pinkies touching, your thumbs out, and other fingers extended. "Keep your elbows in close to your body," says Holt, who led the NFL with 117 catches in 2003.

④ Always reach your hands out toward the ball, and catch it with your fingers away from your body. "Don't let the ball bounce off your palms," says Holt. "You want to have soft hands and cradle the ball." Your arms should give with the ball as you squeeze it tight to your body.

⑤ If you are running a long pass pattern, when you look over your shoulder to see the pass, first locate the nose of the football to determine where the ball is headed. Position your body between the defender and the spot on the field where the ball is going to land. When you are catching the ball on the run and it is coming over your shoulder, reach both hands out, palms up with your pinkies touching, thumbs out, and other fingers extended.

⑥ Focus all of your attention on looking the ball into your hands and making the catch. Try not to "hear the footsteps" of any defenders who are out to get you. "You can't worry about getting hit," says Holt, who has 869 catches for 12,660 yards since turning pro in 1999. "A defender is going to hit you if you catch it, and he's going to hit you if you don't. So you might as well make the catch."

⑦ Once you make the grab, tuck the ball into whichever arm is closer to the sideline to protect it from defenders who will be trying to strip it from you. Secure the ball when you run by placing one end of the ball into the crook of your elbow and clutching the other end with your hand, the nose of the ball between your index and middle fingers. Hold the ball tight against your body. "The defender is going to be clawing for the ball. Use your other arm to stiff-arm him and keep him away from it," says Holt.

Torry Holt was a member of the 1999 Super Bowl–winning St. Louis Rams.

Kicking a Soccer-Style Field Goal

ROBBIE GOULD
2006 Pro Bowl Placekicker

All soccer-style kickers hit the ball with the top of their foot, not their toes.

① Stand over the spot where the ball will be spotted. The ball should be under your right shoulder and your plant foot under your left shoulder. (For a right-footed kicker, the plant foot is your left foot.)

② Take two full steps back from the ball and two three-quarter steps to the left. Get comfortable and stand flat-footed with your plant foot forward, then pick up your plant foot and put it down to move your momentum forward.

③ Take your first step with your kicking foot toward the ball. Extend your left arm for balance. Set your plant foot shoulder-width from the ball as you start the kicking motion. "The higher back you bring your kicking leg, the more power you're going to generate," says Gould, who kicked twenty-six straight field goals for the Chicago Bears in 2006.

④ The toe of your plant foot should face the target, allowing your hips to come through and face straight forward when you kick the ball. Says Gould: "You want a nice, swinging motion through the ball." Your left arm should come across your body to stabilize you and prevent the ball from hooking. Follow through with your kicking leg to finish your motion and to keep the ball on target.

⑤ All soccer-style kickers hit the ball with the top of their foot, not their toes. To make good contact, flex your foot so that your toes are pointing out. Your foot should be perpendicular to the ball, and your foot, ankle, and knee should be straight and locked when you make

contact with the ball. "Your head should be down, looking at the ball the whole time," says Gould, who kicked a 49-yard field goal in overtime to propel the Bears to the 2006 NFC Championship Game. "The crowd lets you know if the kick is good or not."

Robbie Gould has converted 84.8 percent of his field goal attempts entering 2009, making him the second most accurate kicker in NFL history.

Booming a Punt

BRIAN MOORMAN
Two-time Pro Bowl Punter

Quick Tip

Drop the ball gently onto your foot.

① Start in a balanced, comfortable stance. Your legs should be positioned shoulder-width apart, keeping your kicking foot about 6 to 8 inches behind your non-kicking foot. Focus on the long snapper and the ball; don't worry about the defensive rush. "If you muff the snap a turnover can put your team in a hole," says Moorman, a Pro Bowl selection with the Buffalo Bills in 2005 and 2006.

② Prepare to receive the snap with your arms bent in an L shape and your hands out in front of you. Square your body to the line of scrimmage. "Stay square [to the scrimmage line] so if you get a wide snap, you can adjust [to the ball] with a side step," says Moorman.

③ As the ball is snapped, watch the ball all the way into your hands. When you catch the ball, position it in your hands to make sure the laces on the ball are pointing up. "You want the laces up when you drop the ball," he says.

④ Hold the football out in front of your body with both hands. Hold the ball with your fingers, not your palms. Keep the football parallel to the ground and angled slightly left, at about 11 o'clock. "This is so the outside of your foot strikes the ball evenly when you kick it," says Moorman.

⑤ Kick in a three-step motion. To begin kicking, take a small step forward with your non-kicking foot, followed by a medium step with your kicking foot and then a final plant step onto your non-kicking foot. "Firmly plant your foot into the ground," says Moorman. "This will build up the momentum for punting the ball."

⑥ As you begin swinging your kicking leg, slowly remove your non-kicking-side hand from the football. Try to drop the ball gently onto your foot the same way every time. Don't let the ball spin or move, because it will be harder to make solid contact. "Keep your head down," says Moorman, "and kick through the ball."

⑦ When you make contact with the ball, point the toes of your kicking foot away from your body so that the ball hits the top of your foot. "It is the best way for your foot to fit on the football," says Moorman, who has punted more than six hundred times in his career. Punting this way will also cause the ball to spiral and travel farther.

⑧ Your body should finish forward after you kick. Don't fall backward. Spring off your plant foot and try to jump forward into the ball a little bit when you make contact. Then keep walking forward after you kick. "That will keep your leg going in the direction that you are trying to kick," says Moorman.

Fast Fact Brian Moorman has a career punting average of 43.3 yards per punt since 2001.

Long Snapping for a Punt

JAMES DEARTH
NFL Long Snapper

First get in a balanced stance before reaching to grip the football.

① A long snap for a punt travels about 15 yards. It is a two-handed backward spiral pass made from between the legs of a player who is hunched over. "Always use two hands," says Dearth, who has served as the Jets' long snapper on punts and placekicks in every game since 2001. Three key elements to long snapping a football are stance, grip, and delivery.

② To set up in a stance, place each foot about 10 to 12 inches behind the football. Point your toes forward and slightly out. The football should be in front of the snapper's helmet so the player has to reach out for the ball with his arm nearly fully extended. The snapper gets into position by placing his feet slightly wider than shoulder-width apart. Your feet must be wider than your hips, says Dearth, because "the power is going to come from flexing your hips when you snap the ball."

③ The player should make sure to first get into a balanced stance before reaching to grip the ball. If he reaches for the ball while setting his base, his weight will not be well balanced under his hips. "You'll snap the ball and then fall forward," says Dearth, who has appeared in 128 consecutive regular-season games, all with the Jets, entering the 2009 season.

④ As the center sets his feet, Dearth suggests he should bend his knees and transfer his weight back from the balls of his feet onto his heels. "Dig in [to the turf] and get a solid base." Weight distribution and proper knee bend are important to achieve a solid base. For the player to transfer his weight back toward the punter and bend his knees, he must keep his rear end down at all times.

⑤ Once the snapper has established a strong foundation, the player is now ready to grip the football. When reaching for the ball, the player must maintain the proper posture he established in his base. Place your dominant hand on the ball with the laces up. Grip the ball the same way you would to throw a pass. Place your index finger at the top of the laces and wrap your thumb around the ball, resting the other three fingers along the laces.

⑥ With your dominant hand securing the ball, turn your wrist inward toward the inside of your forearm, so that the back of your hand faces the ground. Now place the fingertips of your offhand on the football so you are cradling the ball. "Use your hands to form a cup around the ball," says Dearth. "A good cup will make the ball rotate in a fast, tight spiral when you snap it." Only the fingertips and the inside of your fingers should touch the ball—never your palms.

⑦ When the player is ready to prepare to snap the football, the player ducks his head and looks back at the punter. "Focus on the punter's belt buckle and try to snap the ball directly at it," says Dearth, who has thirty-one career special teams tackles. Look back through your legs without dropping your chest and shoulders. Remember to keep your butt parallel to the ground.

⑧ Snap the football. Don't drag the ball on the ground. Quickly pick up the ball and swing your arms rearward. "When snapping the ball, the player swings his arms backward in one quick, continuous motion," says Dearth. At the same time the player snaps the football, his grip hand and guide hand impart a push/pull pressure on the ball, giving the ball its spiraling action as it exits the snapper's hands and travels backward through the snapper's legs. "What helped me out was that I could throw a football," says Dearth, a former collegiate quarterback at Tulsa who transferred to Tarelton State (Texas) and switched to tight end. "If you can throw a football, you can throw it between your legs."

⑨ As the player releases the ball, he should turn his palms away from each other. The hands and arms continue all the way through the legs until they are fully extended rearward. Finally, the index fingers release the ball and finish directly on line with the center's belt buckle. "Keep your hands near the ground [when snapping the ball], and make sure they go straight back, rather than up [toward your rear end]," says Dearth. If the player's hands rise too high off the ground, the snap will sail high. "They're going to smack you around, and you've got to be able to throw a good snap while they're hitting you," says Dearth. "That's one of the hardest parts of the [snapper's] job."

James Dearth has caught three career passes, including a 1-yard touchdown pass in 2001.

Making a Paper Football

Quick Tip

Flatten your folds for a tighter football.

① Get a piece of loose-leaf paper. Fold the left half of the paper over onto the right, lengthwise. Then fold it lengthwise again.

② Fold the top right corner of the paper down to make a triangle. "I never got a paper cut," says Bettis, who rushed for 13,662 career yards, fifth on the NFL all-time list, with the St. Louis Rams and Pittsburgh Steelers from 1993 to 2006. "I was always agile with making the footballs." Continue folding triangles from the top of the paper. Stop when you have a small "flap" of paper left.

③ Tuck the flap into the pocket left over from the last triangle. Have your friend make a finger goalpost at the far end of a table and try kicking your football through the uprights.

Fast Fact Jerome Bettis was a member of the 2006 Super Bowl champion Pittsburgh Steelers.

Golf

Gripping a Golf Club

DAVID LEADBETTER
Pro Golf Instructor

Hold the club so it feels like a normal extension of your hands.

(1) There are three types of grips most common to golfers: overlapping, interlocking, and baseball. Experiment with each of the three grips and then decide which grip is the best grip for you. Says Leadbetter: "To paraphrase Ben Hogan, 'Good golf begins with a good grip.'" (These directions are for a right-handed golfer. Reverse the hands if you are left-handed.)

(2) The overlapping grip is the most popular way to hold the club, because it offers the best combination of strength and feel. With this grip, the little finger of the right hand overlaps the index finger of the left hand and rests between the index finger and the middle finger of the left hand. "The pinkie of the right hand rides piggyback on top of the index finger of the left hand," says Leadbetter, who over a thirty-year career has coached an illustrious group of pro golfers, including Nick Faldo, Ernie Els, Nick Price, and Michelle Wie.

(3) The interlocking grip provides a stronger hold on the club. With the interlocking grip, the little finger of the right hand is set firmly between the index finger and the middle finger of the left hand, and the index finger of the left hand is set firmly between the last two fingers of the right hand. "There is a line that forms a V between your thumb and first knuckle on either hand," says Leadbetter.

(4) The baseball grip provides maximum feel and hand action and is an ideal grip for youth golfers and hackers who play golf infrequently. There is no interlocking or overlapping with the baseball grip. Instead,

the index finger of the left hand and the little finger of the right hand touch each other, and the thumb of the left hand is set squarely down the middle of the shaft. "It's just one hand beneath the other," says Leadbetter, whose golfers have won more than a dozen major championships and more than one hundred tournaments.

⑤ To grip the club properly, it is important to place the club diagonally in your fingers. A common mistake among golfers is that they take their club from the bag and then grip it and rip it, or they rest the clubhead on the ground and then apply their grip. "People tend to fall into those errors," says Leadbetter. "Apply your grip with the clubhead in the air, so you can feel the weight of the club in your fingers." Whatever grip you are using, the back of your top, or lead, hand and the palm of your bottom hand both are set squarely at the target. "The grip is complex in nature, but it is so important, because the grip determines what happens to the clubface," says Leadbetter. "A good golfer needs to have great hands, and great hands equal a great grip."

⑥ Take the club with your top (left) hand first, resting the butt of the club in your palm, atop the pad at the point where the last two fingers meet. The rest of your top hand should then fall naturally into position across the base of the middle and the index fingers. The thumb of the top hand should be set squarely down the center of the shaft. Next, wrap your bottom (right) hand around the club so that the club rests against your fingers—not against your palm. "A palming grip creates errors," says Leadbetter. "If the club is too much in your palms you'll strangle the club causing tension, and that leads to errors." Put the rest of your hand around the club. Make sure that the thumb and index finger of the bottom hand touch each other once they are in place.

⑦ Once you are gripping the club, don't strangle it. Try to hold the club so it feels like a normal extension of your hands. Grip the club just tightly enough so that you can control the club throughout the swing. "A light grip is the order of the day," says Leadbetter. "Not loose, but light." When holding the club, the last three fingers of the top hand and the middle and ring fingers of the lower hand should exert most of the pressure in the grip.

⑧ During the swing, each hand should supply an equal amount of pressure on the grip. Bad shots happen when one hand exerts too much pressure. Too much pressure by the bottom hand will produce a fast swing, while too much pressure by the top hand will keep the club from reaching its proper backswing. The two hands work as one. Says Leadbetter: "Have a good grip at a young age, and you keep it for life."

 There are currently thirty David Leadbetter Golf Academies in thirteen countries.

Reading the Green

DAVE STOCKTON
Two-time PGA Champion

The putt will always break toward water.

①　To predict how much a putt will break, analyze the contours of the green and decide which way the ball will curve on its way to the hole. "Don't wait until you're already on the green [to start reading it]," says Stockton, winner of the 1970 and 1976 PGA Championship. Pay attention to the green as you approach it from the fairway about 40 yards away. From that distance, you can see the overall slope or tilt of the green.

②　As you approach the green, Stockton says to look for the obvious signs built into every green. The putt will always break toward water, because the green is sloped that way for drainage. If you see a pond to

the left of the green, that's a sign that the green slopes in that direction. "Look to see where water drains off the green, because that's where the ball will go," says Stockton, who has won ten PGA Tour career titles since turning pro in 1964.

③ Be aware of Mother Nature. If there are mountains on the left of the green and an ocean on the right, the prevailing terrain is downhill right, and the putt will break left to right. If you're putting toward mountains, expect the ball to break away from the highest peak. Be aware of golf course design, too, and use common sense. Putts rarely break in the direction of a green-side bunker, because the architect designs the green so that runoff will not flow into the sand.

④ Study the putting line from two directions: from behind the ball and from behind the hole. "Get as low as possible," says Stockton. Crouch down if necessary, because subtle undulations aren't easily seen from a steep angle. Another good vantage point to study the putting line is midway between the ball and the hole. This view tells whether you are putting uphill or downhill, which will determine the speed you putt the ball.

⑤ Another common technique for judging break is the plumb bob. "[This method] is most helpful if you have a five-foot putt and can't determine the break," says Stockton. To plum bob a putt, stand behind the ball and hold your putter like a pendulum, suspended between thumb and index finger, in front of your dominant eye. With the other eye closed, line the shaft up with your ball. If the hole appears on the left side of the shaft, the ground you're standing on slopes left. If the hole appears on the right side of the shaft, it slopes right. No plumb bob is foolproof, Stockton warns: "[Plumb bobbing] tells you which direction the ball will break, but it won't tell you how much."

 Dave Stockton was Ryder Cup captain of the victorious U.S. team in 1991.

Keeping Your Putts on Line

DAVE STOCKTON
Two-time PGA Champion

 Accelerate the putter through the ball.

① To grip the putter, the thumb of your left hand should be set squarely up and down the flat front of the grip. (Lefties should do the opposite.) Then the right thumb should be set in the same position lower on the shaft, with the palm aiming at the target. Your left thumb should be in the groove between your right thumb and right palm. Both thumbs should point straight down. "Grip the club lightly, as if you were holding a bird in your hands and didn't want to hurt it," says Stockton, winner of the 1992 and 1994 Senior Players Championship and the 1996 U.S. Senior Open.

② When your grip is correct, take a practice putt or two. They help you get a feel for how far you are going to take the club back and how far you are going to swing through the ball. Stockton recommends stepping back behind the ball to take your practice strokes. "Don't take practice strokes beside the ball," says Stockton. "Stay behind the ball and take your practice strokes on line with the hole."

③ Stand to address the ball with your feet shoulder-width apart. When your stance and positioning are correct, the ball should be under your dominant eye. Using your practice stroke as a guide, take the club back. Backswings will vary based on the length of the putt. For longer putts, Stockton recommends standing taller in your stance, so you can take the putter back farther and remain balanced.

④ The two keys to successful putting are judging the speed and distance of the putt. "Many golfers get fixated on line, instead of the actual distance the ball needs to roll [to reach the cup]," says Stockton. To help judge a putt's distance, he suggests dividing a putt into thirds, with the last third being when the ball is closest to the hole. "The last third [of the way to the hole] is when your ball is moving slowest and that's when it most likely starts to roll off line," says Stockton, the 1993 Senior Player of the Year.

⑤   To start the putting stroke, move the head of the putter with your shoulders and arms, not your hands. Keep your head down and try to keep the rest of your body still. The face of the putter should be square to the ball. If the face is open (angled away from your body), the ball will drift to the right when you putt. If the face is closed (angled toward your body), the ball will drift left when you putt. "You aren't hitting the ball in the hole," says Stockton. "You are rolling the ball to the hole."

⑥   Don't slow down on impact and jab at the ball. "The worst thing you can do is to leave the putter behind the ball," says Stockton. Make contact with a smooth tempo and accelerate the putter through the ball. As a general rule, your follow-through should be the same length as your backswing. "Think of [your putter] as if it is a paint brush and you are using it to paint with 6- to 8-inch brushstrokes back and forth."

⑦   Like snowflakes, no two putting strokes are the same. Says Stockton: "One of the most important things I've learned is that you don't have methods, you have individuals. You have to feel comfortable over the ball and confident in your putting stroke. If you trust [your stroke], you're going to be a more consistent putter."

Dave Stockton made history in March 1996, when he and his two sons each played a different Tour event on the same weekend: Dave was at the FHP Health Care Classic, Dave Jr. was playing at the Doral-Ryder Open, and Dave's youngest son, Ronnie, was playing in the Inland Empire Open on the Nationwide Tour.

Improving Your Short Game

JUSTIN LEONARD
1997 British Open Champion

Swing through the ball. Take a healthy divot.

① Short iron shots require accuracy, feel, and finesse. The trick is to hit the ball close enough to the hole so that you will have a reasonable putt waiting for you on the green. Getting the ball up and down in two strokes from 50 yards away is what distinguishes the good players from the average. "The trouble with most golfers who hit a pitching wedge is that they don't *hit* the shot," says Leonard. Instead, they flip the ball toward the target with a loose and long swing. The longer the swing, the less feel, touch, and finesse there will be to the shot.

② In setting up, take a stance that is slightly narrower than normal and open it slightly by moving your front foot back a few inches. (That's the left foot for right-handed golfers.) At address, the ball should be in the middle of your stance, and most of your body weight is on your front side. Keep your body movement to a minimum during this shot. Restrict movement by pushing your back knee in a bit and plant the inside of your back foot squarely into the turf. "Work from a solid base," says Leonard, winner of twelve PGA Tour career titles since turning pro in 1994.

③ Take a short, compact swing with plenty of force and feel. Make solid contact with the ball. As you hit it, make certain that you do not collapse your lead elbow. Keep your hands firm, never allowing them to get too loose or wristy, and strike the ball while the face of the club is reaching the end of its downward arc. Then, after impact, swing the club through the ball, taking a healthy divot, and into the follow-through, keeping the clubhead on line with the target. "Don't break down at the wrists," says Leonard.

④ The chip shot from 20 yards off the green is a great stroke saver. In chipping, the trick is to have the ball roll, not fly, as much as possible. It is far easier to control a rolling golf ball than it is to control an airborne one. "So keep [the ball] low," says Leonard, the 1994 NCAA champion. To play the chip shot successfully, you must have a good sense of feel and touch for the shot. You should chip with a five-iron or six-iron.

⑤ To chip, set up in a stance that resembles your putting stance. Be certain to set your hands in front of the ball, because you want to chip the ball while the clubhead is still on its descent. "Shorten up on the grip and play the ball back toward your right foot," says Leonard. The backswing should be short, but you want to strike the ball firmly. It is important to keep your wrist break as minimal as possible during the chip shot. Breaking the wrists on such a short, precise shot often leads to a fluffed shot that travels about three feet.

Fast Fact Justin Leonard won the 1994 Haskins Award as the nation's most outstanding college golfer while attending the University of Texas.

Escaping a Sand Trap

GARY PLAYER

Hall of Fame Golfer

Aim to miss the ball and hit the sand.

① Hitting out of a sand trap looks harder than it actually is. "The sand shot is not nearly as difficult as it may seem and is one that should not be feared," says Player, who was inducted into the World Golf Hall of Fame in 1974. Practice this shot tirelessly. "It is the best way to become a great bunker player."

② Set up by digging your feet into the sand to create a stable base; you don't want to slip in a bunker. Adopt a stance that is just a bit wider than your normal one. Your feet are now in the sand, slightly below the level of the ball, so shorten up on the club. Choke down on the sand wedge so that your bottom hand is about an inch from the bottom of the grip. Make sure that your body and grip are relaxed.

③ When playing the green-side bunker shot, address the ball with an open stance, turning your lead foot toward the target on the green. Set up so the ball is slightly inside your front heel and your hands are forward, opposite your front leg. The length of the backswing is determined in part by the distance between your ball and the target. The shorter the shot, the deeper you dig the clubface into the sand; the longer the shot, the shallower you dig into the sand. "The problem that most amateurs have is 'taking too much sand' or 'digging too deep,'" says Player, winner of nine major PGA Tour championships.

④ Take a backswing so that the end of the grip is pointed toward the ball. Your front arm will be parallel to the ground. You should use about double the swing force you would apply to a regular pitch shot from a similar distance. After reaching the top of your backswing, accelerate the club toward the sand. Strike the club into the sand approximately one full ball length behind your ball. By doing this, you allow the clubface to cut through the sand and pop the ball out of the bunker. Don't baby the swing. "Keep one prevailing thought in mind," says Player. "'Strike the match.' The downswing is the key and like striking a match it implies a firm, crisp action. If you strike the match too hard the head breaks off. If you strike it too slowly—deceleration—the match does not light."

⑤ Keep your eyes focused on the point at which you want the clubface to enter the sand. Remember to accelerate through the ball. This acceleration will also allow you to glide the clubhead through the sand and to finish the swing. If you are not accelerating the clubhead, you will more than likely not have enough momentum to knock the ball onto the green. Says Player: "When the club decelerates, the wrists roll over and the clubface digs into the sand."

⑥ When you initially make contact with the sand, your wrists will have a tendency to bend due to the resistance of the sand. To overcome this resistance, focus on keeping your wrists firm until after you get through the sand. Be sure to keep the face of your sand wedge open throughout the entire swing. If you don't, the clubhead will burrow into the sand and turn in, and as a result the ball will fail to leave the sand. "Suddenly you are at bogey instead of putting for birdie," says Player, a three-time Masters champion (1961, '74, '78), two-time PGA Champion (1962, '72), and winner of the 1965 U.S. Open. To keep the clubface open, make certain that your top hand never passes over or even across the bottom hand at impact.

⑦ After striking the ball, it is important to follow through completely with a good hip and shoulder turn. "Striking the match means swinging crisply through the sand," says Player, the only golfer in the modern era to have won the British Open in three different decades (1959, '68, and '74). "This allows your wrists to release automatically and results in a full follow-through, thus avoiding the dreaded deceleration."

⑧ Aim just to the left of the target if you are right-handed, and just to the right if you are left-handed. As you swing back toward the ball you should feel as if you're cutting across the ball, from outside to in. While this may feel unnatural, trust your swing. "Trust your natural swing and practice relentlessly to master it," says Player. Even though you think you're going to hit the ball too far left (if you are right-handed), the fact that your clubface is open will actually take the ball to the right. "Practice until you can't hit another ball," says Player. "The harder you practice the luckier you get."

Gary Player achieved the career grand slam on both the PGA Tour and the Seniors Tour. He has won 164 world golf titles, including eighteen major world championships.

Ice Hockey

Snapping a Wrist Shot

CHRIS DRURY

1999 NHL Rookie of the Year

Quickly snap your wrists to release the shot.

① Successful goal-scorers usually have an effective wrist shot because it is the most accurate way to shoot and can be released quickly. Start with your feet shoulder-width apart and your weight on your back leg. Position your body at a 45-degree angle to the net, lowering your shoulder as you reach back and down with your stick to position the puck.

② Your hands should be a little more than body-width apart and your lower hand should be halfway down the shaft of the stick "where you can get leverage," says Drury, currently captain of the New York Rangers. The puck should be at the center of your stick blade and in line with your back foot.

③ As you begin to sweep the puck forward, shift your weight toward your front leg and rotate your body forward. Keep your eyes locked on the target. "With a wrist shot, for the most part, you're never looking down at the puck," says Drury, a member of the 2001 Stanley Cup–winning Colorado Avalanche.

④ As you are sliding the puck forward on the ice, when the stick blade crosses your body, transfer your body weight on your stick while pushing forward with your lower hand and down with your top hand.

⑤ Once the puck is between your legs, quickly snap your wrists to release the shot. The puck is released when it reaches your front foot and your shoulders are square to the net. At the point of release, your wrists turn, causing the stick blade to turn out and lift the puck.

⑥ Follow through by "pointing the stick where you want the puck to go," says Drury. "If you want to shoot it high, follow through high." The height of the shot also depends on how much you rotate your wrists.

Chris Drury led his hometown of Trumbull, Connecticut, to the Little League Baseball World Series championship in 1989.

Shooting a Slap Shot

JASON ARNOTT
Two-time NHL All-Star

Quick Tip

It's important to twist your hips when shooting a slap shot.

(1) Hold the stick the same way you would for a wrist shot. Make sure that your bottom hand is about halfway down the stick. This will help you flex the stick when you shoot and whip the puck forward.

(2) The puck should be between your legs, 2 feet away from your body. Your eyes should be looking down at the puck and your weight should be on your back leg.

③ Start the shot by bringing your stick back so the blade is in line with your back shoulder. In general, you should not bring your stick past shoulder height. If you take too big a windup, the defense will have more time to prepare to block the shot.

④ As you bring your stick forward, shift your weight toward your front leg. It's also important to twist your hips back when you start the shot and twist them forward as you bring your stick down. "The hips are where you generate the most power on a slap shot," says Arnott, captain of the NHL's Nashville Predators.

⑤ The puck should be lined up a little inside your front foot. Your stick blade should make contact with the ice approximately 3 inches behind the puck. "You want the stick to hit the ice right before the puck so you get the most power," says Arnott, whose slap shot clocked 100.3 miles per hour at the 2008 All-Star Hardest Shot Competition.

⑥ After you make contact with the puck, snap your wrists. Follow through with your stick pointing toward the target. "Follow through so that the toe of your stick is pointed where you want the puck to end up," says Arnott. "Remember to roll your wrists as you follow through."

Jason Arnott scored the Stanley Cup–winning overtime goal for the 2000 New Jersey Devils.

Winning More Face-Offs

KRIS DRAPER

Center, Detroit Red Wings

Use more than just your stick to win a face-off.

① Winning face-offs is important. When you win a face-off, your team controls the puck. "Your team is going to win a lot of games if you can keep the puck away from [your opponent]," says Draper, a member of four Stanley Cup–winning Detroit teams.

② Winning face-offs requires a combination of reflexes and timing. The players who are the best in the face-off circle are the ones who always make contact with the puck during a face-off. "Never lose a face-off without at least touching the puck," says Draper.

③ Pull the puck back when taking an offensive zone face-off. Many young players want to push the puck past the other player, or try to go around the opponent and shoot on goal. This usually results in a turnover. Instead, pull the puck back to a defenseman and let your team set up for a great scoring opportunity. "Draw the puck back to your defense," says Draper, "and head to the front of the net."

④ When there is a tie-up in the face-off circle, use more than just your stick to win a face-off. "Kick the puck if you have to," says Draper, who has played in more than one thousand games with the Red Wings since 1993. If he is unable to free his stick, Draper will often take his left hand off the stick, reach down, and push the puck back to his defense with his glove.

⑤ When taking defensive zone face-offs, especially during the penalty kill, Draper recommends being as tenacious and creative as possible. As the puck is dropped, Draper will often rotate his body counterclockwise

so that his right foot slides into the face-off circle and cuts his opponent's stick off from the puck. This allows Draper to stick the puck back to his defenseman for a clearing opportunity.

⑥ Be unpredictable. If you take several face-offs during a game, vary your style. "You don't want to do the same thing over and over again," says Draper. "Eventually, [your opponent] is going to figure out what you're doing and is going to counter."

Kris Draper won the 2004 Selke Trophy as the National Hockey League's best defensive forward.

MINDING YOUR NET

ED BELFOUR
Two-time Vezina Trophy Winner (NHL's Top Goaltender)

A goaltender's stick should always be on the ice.

① Get in a ready position with your head up. Stand with your feet a little wider than shoulder-width apart and your skates parallel to each other. Bend your knees slightly inward, keeping your weight on the inside edges of the balls of your feet "so you can move faster and react quicker to shots," says Belfour, winner of the Vezina Trophy for goalie of the year after the 1991 and 1993 seasons.

② In a proper stance, your shoulders are level and your chest is square to the shooter. "You want the shooter to be able to see the logo of your jersey," says Belfour. Your catching glove should be open and a bit out in front of your body. "The only time your glove should be closed is when the puck is in it," says Belfour, whose 484 career wins rank third on the all-time list. Your blocker should also be held out in front of your body. "Hold your glove and blocker at the same height." The glove and blocker should be held slightly outside and above the goaltender's hips with elbows slightly outside the body to cover the widest goal area possible. On shots in tight a goaltender should bring elbows in and to the side of the body, eliminating any holes and forming a wall. "Be as compact as possible."

③ An ice hockey goaltender's stick should always be on the ice. Even when moving from side to side or post to post, keep your stick on the ice at all times. Place your stick about 10 inches in front of your feet so the stick doesn't get tangled in your skates. This also allows for some cushioning when blocking harder shots. Belfour suggests holding the

stick at a slight open angle to your glove side "so a rebound caroms to that side and away from the front of the crease."

④ Follow the action with your eyes, but keep your body still and in control before the shot. "In the ideal situation, you'd like to be in a stopped position so you can react," says the six-time All-Star. To make a skate save, turn your skate outward while you slide your skate out to the side in a kicking motion toward the corner. A goalie's legs and arms move independently. "When you move your legs, your arms don't move with them," says Belfour.

⑤ Use the butterfly position to cover both low corners at the same time. A butterfly save is most effective when trying to stop low shots, screened shots, or shots from close range. When dropping into a butterfly position, the goaltender should quickly drive his knees onto the ice. Push your feet out to the sides to cover the maximum amount of net possible. "A common mistake [in the butterfly position] is lifting your stick off the ice and not covering the five-hole," says Belfour, referring to the open space between a goalie's legs. Another mistake is extending the stick too far out in front of the goaltender's knees. This creates an angled stick much like a ramp that will direct the puck over the goaltender's shoulder and into the net.

(6) When extending the leg pads to the sides, make sure the inside of the pads are flush on the ice and your knees are together. "Keeping your butt up will help keep your knees on the ice," says Belfour. This will also help the goalie recover and gain proper positioning. After you've gone down in the butterfly position and made the save, quickly get back up. It's more difficult to move side to side from your knees than it is on your feet. Get back up using one leg at a time. "Get up on the leg farthest away from the puck first," says Belfour, the 1991 NHL Rookie of the Year.

(7) Pay attention to the shooter's tendencies and read the situation. "Know if the shooter is left-handed or right-handed. Try to pick up the puck as quickly as you can." When the puck is shot, you'll be ready to make the save. If the puck is not in your glove after the shot, locate it as soon as possible. If it was deflected, you need to find it and cover any open parts of the net. Belfour recommends playing other sports to improve agility and other important goaltending skills. "Playing soccer is good," Belfour says, "because we use our feet a fair amount."

 Ed Belfour played for five NHL teams from 1989 to 2008. He was a member of the 1999 Stanley Cup champion Dallas Stars.

Skating Backward on Defense

TOM POTI
NHL Defenseman

Make sure to look over both shoulders when you're skating in reverse.

① Balance is a must in skating backward. "You need steadiness [to skate backward]," says Poti, who has played for four teams since joining the National Hockey League in 1998. For a balanced base, position your legs shoulder-width apart. Keeping your upper body from tipping forward will also help you remain steady.

② To skate backward, move one leg in an arc, or C-shape, along the side of your body. As you are bringing that leg back under you, start to

make an arc with your other leg. To create more power, make those arcs wider and dig the inside edge of your skate blade into the ice. "Try to grab as much ice as you can," says Poti, a member of the silver medal–winning 2002 U.S. Olympic hockey team. "The more you grab the more speed you'll pick up."

③ Knowing where you're going is an important thing while skating backward. Make sure to look over both your shoulders when you're skating in reverse. "You don't want to only look over one shoulder all the time because then you're missing half the ice," says Poti.

 Tom Poti was named to the NHL All-Rookie team after the 1998-99 season.

Taping a Hockey Stick for a Better Grip

ERIC DESJARDINS
Retired NHL Defenseman

Try using more or less tape until you get the right feel.

① Get a roll of gauze tape, which you can buy at a drugstore. Says Desjardins: "It's really thin, it's got some stickiness to it, and it's stretchy."

② You're going to wrap the tape around the stick at four different spots. Start with the butt end. Begin by wrapping the tape twenty times around the end of the stick to make a knob.

③ Cut the tape and seal the cut piece down. Move a quarter inch down the shaft and begin winding the tape again. Wrap it fifteen times and seal.

④ Move down the shaft another quarter inch and wind again, wrapping the tape fifteen times. Move down once more and wrap the tape one final time. That grip "gives me a nice handle," says Desjardins, who played seventeen seasons with the Montreal Canadiens and Philadelphia Flyers from 1988 to 2006. "My fingers fit in the gaps between the tape. The feel I get is perfect."

 Eric Desjardins scored three goals for the Montreal Canadiens in Game 2 of the 1993 Stanley Cup finals, the only hat trick by a defenseman in Stanley Cup finals history.

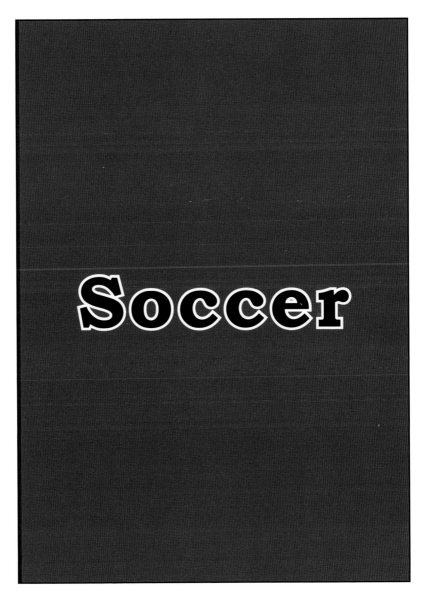

Soccer

Blasting a Goal Kick

TONY MEOLA
Major League Soccer's All-Time Saves Leader

Run up to the ball with long, smooth strides.

① When taking a goal kick, don't place the ball on just any spot. "Make sure you put the ball on a nice piece of grass, so it comes off your foot clean," says Meola, the holder of Major League Soccer goal-keeping records for most career saves, most saves in a game, and most shutouts in a season.

② Set up seven or eight paces behind the ball. To make it possible to strike the ball with maximum power, don't take short, choppy steps to the ball. "Run up to the ball with long, smooth strides," he says.

③ Swing your kicking leg back as far as possible. "The farther back your leg, the more leg speed, the more power you'll generate coming forward [into the ball]." Approach the ball from a 45-degree angle. "Opening up your hips will also increase [your power]," Meola says.

④ To execute a goal kick with the proper trajectory and distance, you want to drive the lower half of the ball using your upper instep, not the top of your shoelaces. "[This is how] a goal kick is different from shooting [on goal]," he says. A right-footed kicker, Meola points the toes of his right foot slightly outward in order to get his kicking foot under the lower half of the ball. "Think of your [kicking] foot as a golf wedge getting under the ball."

⑤ As you step into the kick, your plant foot should be slightly bent and about 10 inches behind the ball. "If your [plant foot is] too close to the ball, you won't get any height on the kick," says the five-time All-Star.

As you make contact with the ball, keep the ankle of your kicking foot locked and be sure to follow through straight at the target area.

⑥ Like most goalkeepers, Meola tries to kick the ball at least 15 feet above the ground, so an opponent can't block it. Being able to kick the ball high and far is an important part of a goalkeeper's game. If executed properly, says Meola, "a great goal kick can turn into instant offense."

 Tony Meola made one hundred appearances in goal for the U.S. national team between 1988 and 2006.

Converting a Penalty Shot

HEATHER O'REILLY
Olympic Gold Medalist

 Don't reveal where you are going to kick the ball.

(1) Scoring on a penalty kick is not as easy as it seems. "Confidence is important," says O'Reilly. "If you believe you'll make [the kick], you probably will."

(2) Place the ball on the penalty spot. Remove any debris that could cause the ball to fly off course. Stay calm and breathe normally. "Have only positive thoughts," says O'Reilly, a member of the 2004 and 2008 U.S. Olympic gold medal–winning teams.

(3) Don't reveal where you are going to kick the ball. The goalkeeper is likely to be watching your eyes for clues, so once you decide which corner to aim at, don't look at that corner. You might look to the right corner but plan to kick the ball to the left corner. Says O'Reilly: "Keep the goalkeeper guessing."

(4) Take a deep breath and start to run toward the ball. A common mistake made by young players is that they watch the goalkeeper's movement and then try to decide whether the goalkeeper will dive to the left or to the right. "Whatever you do, don't change your mind [about where you will shoot] at this point," says O'Reilly, a U.S. national team member since 2002. Ignore any distracting shouts from opposing players.

(5) As you approach the ball to shoot, position your plant foot a couple of feet behind the ball, pointing toward your target. "If your plant foot is too close [to the ball], you won't get much power. Too far, and you'll be reaching."

⑥ Your chin and chest should be over the ball when you make contact to prevent the ball from sailing too high. By leaning your body forward you will be able to keep your kick low to the ground. The ankle of your kicking foot should be locked. When she's close to the goal, O'Reilly prefers to kick the ball with the inside of her foot, near her arch. "I have more control, and I can put the ball in either corner."

⑦ Your foot should strike the middle of the ball to generate the most pace. "That's the sweet spot," says O'Reilly, who scored the winning goal for Sky Blue FC in the 2009 Women's Professional Soccer championship game. Follow through so that you land on your kicking foot after the shot.

⑧ Try to place the ball about 3 feet from either post. The goalkeeper will be standing on the goal line in the center of the goal area, so it will be difficult for the goalie to defend the area beside each post. If you shoot the ball with power, low to the ground, and with accuracy, you will surely score a goal.

Heather O'Reilly was a member of the 2003 and 2006 NCAA champion North Carolina Tar Heels.

Bending it like Beckham

BRAD DAVIS
Two-time MLS All-Star

Put spin on the ball by striking the side of the ball just off center.

(1) How do you make a shot bend? By putting spin on the ball. This shooting technique is used when you want to curve the ball around a defensive wall on a free kick from beyond the 18-yard line.

(2) Start by placing the ball on the ground. "Make sure the ball is sitting up nicely," says Davis, a member of the 2006 and 2007 MLS Cup–winning Houston Dynamo. Before kicking the ball, watch how the opponent's wall sets up and try to exploit a weakness. "Check to see if some players [in the wall] are shorter [than others]," says Davis, "and send the ball over their heads."

(3) You'll also want to check the positioning of the goalkeeper. "Look where the goalkeeper is to see if he can read where you're going to kick the ball," says Davis. If the goalie is on the right side, aim left, and vice versa. "Don't give [the goalie] any clues about where you are going to kick the ball."

(4) To set up, step back several feet and approach the ball from a 45-degree angle. Right-footed shooters should step back to their left. Lefty shooters, like Davis, should step back to their right. "Close the angle as you approach the ball," he says.

(5) Move forward quickly and set your plant foot about 6 inches behind and to the side of the ball. Make sure to keep your supporting foot steady and pointing toward the goal as you kick the ball. "The ball will fly where your plant foot is pointing," says Davis, who turned pro in 2002.

⑥ Draw back your kicking leg and strike the right side of the ball just off center. If you are left-footed, strike the ball's left side. Provide the ball with spin as your kick it. "[Make contact with] the ball on top of your big toe and [midway between] the side of your shoe and the shoelaces," says Davis.

⑦ As you follow through, your kicking leg should sweep toward the hip of your supporting leg and finish at waist level. "Bend your body back a little to force the ball to lift," says Davis. To stay balanced, extend your opposite arm over your non-kicking leg.

⑧ The right-to-left spin of the ball will bend it to the left. Lefties will spin the ball left to right and bend it to the right. "Try to provide enough spin on the ball to get it away from the goalkeeper," says Davis. The farther you are from the goal line, the harder you can hit the ball. Also keep in mind that a longer distance gives the ball more time to curve.

Fast Fact Brad Davis netted the winning penalty kick in the U.S. shoot-out victory over Panama in the 2005 Gold Cup final.

Improving Your Header

BRIAN McBRIDE

Captain, 2008 U.S. Olympic Soccer Team

Always hit the ball with your forehead.

① Practice with a light ball, such as a beach ball, indoor soccer ball, or soft volleyball, and gradually move on to a regulation soccer ball. "You want to make sure the ball isn't going to hit you on the nose," says McBride, who has made ninety-six appearances for the U.S. squad in international competition.

② Arch your back as the ball approaches, with your chin inward, neck firm, and legs bent. Place your feet a little more than shoulder-width apart. Keep your arms out to your sides for balance and to fend off defenders.

③ You can't head the ball if you can't see it, so keep your eyes open as you get ready to hit the ball. "Seeing the ball helps you control where you're heading it," says McBride, a seven-time Major League Soccer All-Star and the 1998 MLS All-Star Game most valuable player.

④ Always hit the ball with your forehead. "It's the hardest part of your head," says McBride, "and it gives you the most power." Avoid making contact with the top of your head because then it will be difficult to control the direction of the ball.

⑤ When you make contact, snap your upper body toward the ball from the waist. "The strength of the header comes from the waist," says McBride, currently with the Chicago Fire. Drive your head and neck forward as you make contact. Move your head from back to front, not side to side. Follow through by continuing to drive your head forward. Keep both feet on the ground (unless you need to jump to reach the ball).

⑥ If you need to jump, make contact with the ball at the highest point of your jump. When you go up for the ball, try to lift your elbows so that they are parallel to your shoulders. Having your elbows out allows you to keep space between you and your opponent. "Your elbows can also protect you from smacking heads with somebody," says McBride.

 Brian McBride played for the U.S. national team at three World Cups (1998, 2002, and 2006). He is the only American ever to score a goal in more than one World Cup.

Headbanger's Ball

When heading the ball to score a goal, direct the ball down to make it harder for the goalkeeper to save. Direct the ball down by making contact with your head slightly closer to the top of the ball.

To clear the ball from your own goal area, direct the ball up and out. Make contact slightly lower on the ball to send it upward.

Saving a Direct Kick

JOHN BUSCH
2008 MLS Goalkeeper of the Year

Get your body behind the ball in case it slips through your hands.

① Set up in an alert, ready position. "A free kick is a good scoring opportunity for your opponent, especially if the foul occurred near your goal," says Busch, currently playing with the Chicago Fire. Stand with your feet shoulder-width apart, knees slightly bent, and your weight on the balls of your feet. Your hands should be at waist height with your arms bent and the palms of your hands facing each other.

② Carefully watch as your opponent sets up to shoot. "It's surprising how many players look [at the spot] where they're going to shoot," says Busch. Before your opponent approaches the ball, try to read for subtle clues that might help you determine the direction of the shot. "Left-footed kickers like to [kick] to their right, because it's easier to turn on the ball." Your opponent's plant foot is also an important key. The direction the plant foot points is generally the same direction of the shot.

③ When the ball is shot, your body weight should be leaning slightly forward. To block the ball, loosely touch your thumbs together and position your hands to form a W shape behind the ball, not on top of it. "You want to block the ball about a yard in front of your body," says Busch, winner of sixty career games, fourty six by shutout.

④ Never direct the ball back to the shooter or into the middle of the field. To help prevent a rebound, take your first step toward the ball at a 45-degree angle. "You want to prevent second [scoring] chances," says Busch. The best way to avoid a rebound is to punch the ball to the side. This also gives you time to regroup before the next shot on goal.

⑤ When catching the ball, one of the most important fundamentals to remember is watching the ball into your hands. "It's amazing the number of goalies, even professionals, who take their eyes off the ball," says Busch. Try to catch the ball with one hand behind the ball and the other hand on top of the ball. "If you catch the ball cleanly, you have the help of a third hand, which is the ground," says Busch, a 2004 All-Star with the Columbus Crew. Also, try to get your body behind the ball so it can serve as yet another barrier in case the ball slips through your hands.

⑥ Don't be so dramatic. Diving to make a save is sometimes necessary, but don't go overboard with a wild, head-over-heels leap. When jumping for a high ball over your head, always jump while bending one knee in front of your body. "Man, you've got to protect yourself [from injury]," says Busch.

 John Busch had an eighteen-game undefeated streak while playing with the Columbus Crew in 2004.

Stopping a Breakaway

MATT REIS
Four-time MLS All-Star

Wait for the offensive player to push the ball forward to make your move.

① Know when to come out and challenge a breakaway. Proper starting position is crucial. "Leave [the goal area] too soon," says Reis, "and you're [stranded] in no-man's land."

② If the offensive player in control of the ball is within shooting range (about 50 feet away for young players), then the goalkeeper should remain positioned a few feet in front of the goal line to defend against a shot.

③ If the attacker is dribbling the ball toward you in a one-on-one breakaway situation, don't stand on the goal line waiting to react to your opponent. Be aggressive, and limit the offensive player's options. "Run at [the attacker]," says Reis, currently playing with the New England Revolution. "You make the first move."

④ Run at the opponent and approach in a low, ready position. Reis recommends staying on your feet as long as possible to block the shooting angle. "The closer you are to the shooter, the harder it is to get the ball past you [into the net]," he says.

⑤ Timing is a critical element in quashing a breakaway. "Be ready to charge the moment the attacker makes a mistake," says Reis, a two-time Goalkeeper of the Year award finalist. Don't second-guess yourself once you've committed to running at the opponent. "Come hard, and don't stop."

⑥ Wait for the offensive player to push the ball too far forward to make your move. "Don't dive headfirst," says Reis, a member of the 2002

MLS Cup–winning Los Angeles Galaxy. Slide on your side with your body angled across the field, square to the shooter, with your arms outstretched. "Be as big [a blockade] as possible."

⑦ When the moment is right, grab the ball and pull it into your midsection. Try to get the ball when it is as far away from the attacker's foot as possible. Saving a breakaway will surely turn the momentum to your team. "It's a game-changing play," says Reis. "All it takes is a little courage and toughness."

Fast Fact Matt Reis was goalkeeper for the 1997 NCAA champion UCLA Bruins.

Tennis

Serving an Ace

JAMES BLAKE
Pro Tennis Player

Toss the ball an arm's length in front of the baseline.

① Position yourself at the baseline; your feet should be shoulder-width apart with your front foot pointing toward the ad or deuce court that you are serving to. "Before the toss, many players bounce the ball to stay loose," says Blake, winner of ten career singles titles since turning pro in 1999. Develop a pre-toss routine and stick with it.

② As you prepare for the toss, don't squeeze the ball when you hold it. Gently cradle the ball between your thumb and index and middle fingers. Drag your racket backward in a sweeping motion. Toss the ball at this point.

③ Keep your arm straight and toss the ball in the air with your left hand (lefties should do the opposite). "Don't bend your elbow on the toss," says Blake. Finish the toss with your fingers pointing skyward. "You don't really toss the ball so much as let go of it."

④ Toss the ball an arm's length in front of the baseline. "Don't toss the ball too high, because it's hard to time your serve," says Blake. The ball should be just high enough to hit the center of your racket strings when your arm is extended to its highest point.

⑤ Once the ball is in the air, slide your back foot toward your front foot, bend your knees, and then rise up as you prepare to make contact with the ball. Keeping your eye on the ball, rotate your shoulders, and drop the racket behind you as you prepare to uncoil the serve. "Coaches say to scratch your back with the racket head," says Blake.

⑥ It is easier and more accurate to serve with the open face of your racket pointing straight at the net. As you rise up and slightly forward to hit the ball, "throw your racket head at the ball on contact," says Blake, who reached a career-high number-four world ranking in 2006. Follow through so that the racket ends up next to your left leg.

⑦ As soon as you are done serving, says Blake, "Pop up as quickly as possible so you are ready for the return." But of course there won't be one. "Pump your fist then," says Blake, "and score [the point]."

James Blake reached the U.S. Open quarterfinal round in 2005 and 2006.

Returning a Speedy Serve

MELANIE OUDIN

Pro Tennis Player

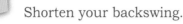

Shorten your backswing.

① You've really got two choices when facing an opponent with a speedy serve. You can either move back behind the baseline to buy yourself more time, or you can stand in and hit a simple block return. "The problem with [standing farther back] is that the server will slice the serve out wide, pushing you off the court," says Oudin, a 2009 U.S. Open quarterfinalist.

② The block return is a good choice, especially if you have quick reflexes. You obviously don't have time to take a big swing at the ball. The ball is traveling faster than a typical shot, so you only have time for a shorter backswing. "Normally when you swing from the baseline, you take your racket all the way back," says Oudin, who turned pro in 2008. "The key [here] is to condense your swing."

③ As the server tosses the ball, take a small two-footed hop forward so that both feet land together shoulder-width apart, heels slightly off the ground. This split step enables you to move quickly in any direction. As the ball is coming at you, don't prepare for a full swing. A short, compact backswing is all that's required. "Just turning your shoulders will do it," says Oudin.

④ The abbreviated swing is achieved by placing your elbows close in to the side of your hips instead of out in front of you. This will shorten your backswing, but you can still hit a strong shot because you're using the server's pace to send the ball back along the same line. "[The technique for hitting] a block return is similar to [the technique for hitting] a volley," says Oudin.

⑤ Hold the racket well out in front of you in a blocking position. Keep a solid wrist and meet the ball with an abbreviated swing in front of your body, transferring your weight forward, as if you're leaning into a strong wind. "When you lean forward into the return and are aggressive, you are taking the server's pace and using it to your advantage," she says. "You're also sending your body in the right direction. When you move backward and play defensively, you're not getting as much power."

⑥ Your return will set the tone for the point, so make sure you are focused when your opponent is preparing to serve the ball. "When you really concentrate, you can read the ball and its spin as it comes to your racket," says Oudin. "Also, concentrate on [your opponent's] tendencies throughout the match. For example, if [your opponent] serves wide all match, before long you're going to lean in that direction and hit a better return."

Melanie Oudin defeated three seeded players to reach the quarterfinals of the 2009 U.S. Open.

Swinging a Two-Handed Backhand

MELANIE OUDIN
Pro Tennis Player

Think of the shot as a forehand hit with your non-dominant hand.

① In the proper stance, your body is well balanced and square to the net, elbows and knees slightly bent, and racket in front of you. Keep your head up and your eyes focused on the ball.

② A right-handed player, Oudin gently supports the throat of the racket with her non-dominant (left) hand until she sees that her next shot will be a backhand. At this point, she is ready to step forward with her right foot. (Left-handed players step forward with their left foot.) As she steps forward, her dominant (right) hand adopts her preferred backhand grip with the palm almost on top of the grip. At the same time, her non-dominant (left) hand slides down the racket handle close to her dominant hand. "Take the racket back by rotating your hips and shoulders away from the net," says Oudin. "If you've got a logo on the front of your shirt, hide it from your opponent."

③ To start the swing, step toward your target, keeping your arms slightly away from your body. Start to shift your weight to your right leg so you can get forward momentum into the shot. Accelerate the head of the racket as you swing through the ball. Extend your non-dominant arm straight out through the ball, making contact just in front of your leading leg. The right knee is slightly flexed.

④ At contact, keep your arms straight. Keep the racket face perfectly level when striking the ball. Keep your wrist solid to avoid a backhand that is too wristy. "You want to drive through the ball [on a two-handed backhand]," says Oudin, who reached the fourth round of Wimbledon in 2009. Strive to achieve full extension with your left arm at contact. When the player has driven through the ball, his left arm should come through fully extended as if he has just hit a lefty forehand. (The opposite is true for left-handed players.)

⑤ Players who hit a two-handed backhand should finish with their chest facing the net and the racket wrapped around their shoulders. Make sure you have a full follow-through out to the target area before you wrap your racket around your shoulder. At the end of the stroke, "your elbows should be bent and pointing at the net and the racket head should be over your shoulder," says Oudin.

⑥ Your back foot should come around with the hips after contact, so your feet and shoulders finish up fairly square to the net. Inexperienced players have trouble opening up their hips and shoulders on the two-handed backhand and end up with their weight on the back foot. Once the left foot plants on the court, "be ready to move back into position toward the center of the court," says Oudin.

⑦ If your shots lack depth, lower your racket head and hit low-to-high on the forward swing. If your shots lack power, "make sure you're not making contact too far in front of your front leg," says Oudin. Once you're comfortable with the shot, make greater use of your non-dominant hand. "Think of the shot as a forehand hit with your [non-dominant] hand," says Oudin. In other words, if you're right-handed, think of it as hitting left-handed forehands with your right hand gently supporting the racket.

Melanie Oudin is the third highest ranked American tennis player after Venus and Serena Williams.

Landing a Topspin Lob

BRAD GILBERT
Pro Tennis Coach

Aim for the baseline over your opponent's backhand side.

① Topspin creates a forward spin that causes the ball to rotate in a bottom-over-top manner. Topspin is applied by drawing the racket strings up and over the ball at the moment of impact. A shot hit with topspin is more likely to stay in play because the ball drops sharply onto the court after reaching its highest point. "Topspin also causes the ball to bounce higher off the ground," says Gilbert, a coach to Andre Agassi, Andy Roddick, and Andy Murray.

② Start your backswing with the racket about one foot below where you would strike the ball if hitting one of your usual ground strokes. Keep the racket face closed. "Use a closed grip so the strings are parallel to the ground," says Gilbert, winner of twenty career titles as a player between 1982 and 1995. To ensure your grip is correct, the palm of your hand should be facing down during the backswing. Your hand and wrist should be relaxed to produce good racket-head speed.

③ Start swinging from below your intended contact point, brushing the racket strings up the back of the ball at the point of contact to generate the required spin. Slightly tilt up the racket strings to give the shot more height. Many players lean on their back foot to create this tilt.

④ Swing through the ball from low to high as your weight is being transferred to your front foot. It takes practice to master this shot. "It's important to have good timing and good balance [when hitting a topspin lob]," says Gilbert. "You don't want to be falling backward."

⑤ Make contact with the ball between waist and shoulder level. Aim to hit the ball at least 5 feet above the net and 3 feet inside the

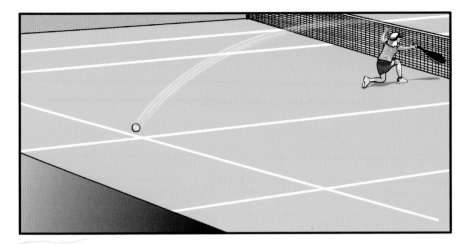

opponent's baseline. Finish your swing by extending the racket over your opposite shoulder, says Gilbert, "just like you would [when] hitting any good passing shot."

⑥ There are two kinds of lobs: the defensive lob and the offensive lob. The objective of the defensive lob is to buy yourself time to get back into position to hit the next shot. By throwing up a defensive lob you are increasing your chances of getting back into the point. "Don't hit a dying quail that [your opponent] can smash back at you," says Gilbert. Hit a high and deep topspin lob, aiming for the far baseline over your opponent's backhand side. If you succeed in making your opponent run back to the baseline, go on the counterattack and charge toward the net.

⑦ Use the offensive topspin lob when your opponent is already in a strong position at the net or closing fast toward the net. "It's devastating to be charging the net and then see a lob go over your head," says Gilbert. "It's the worst feeling." It's always better to hit a lob *too* deep rather than allow your opponent to smash an easy overhead. "At least make [your opponent] hit a tough backhand overhead."

Brad Gilbert won a bronze medal in men's singles at the 1988 Seoul Summer Olympic Games.

Hitting a Feathery Drop Shot

BRAD GILBERT
Pro Tennis Coach

Hit a drop shot in the service box farthest from your opponent.

① A drop shot is a stroke in which the ball is hit lightly enough to barely clear the net; it is designed to catch your opponent off guard when he is far from the net. "[The drop shot] is a crafty play that looks easier than it is," says Gilbert, who reached a career-high number-four world ranking in 1990. "To hit a good one, you need nice touch and good hands."

② The keys to hitting an effective drop shot are disguise and positioning. Always be in an attacking position to hit a drop shot. "Play an *offensive* drop shot," says Gilbert. "It has a higher percentage for success." Don't hit a drop shot from the baseline because the ball must travel a long distance to cross the net. This gives your opponent ample time to react. The best position from which to hit a drop shot is when you are near the service line.

③ To keep from telegraphing your shot, bring the racket back as if you are going to hit a normal forehand ground stroke. "Use the element of surprise," says Gilbert. "The longer you can make it look like a regular shot, the better."

④ Turn your shoulders less than half of the way when preparing the racket for the backswing, depending on where you are on the court. "The closer you are to the net, the less backswing you'll need," says Gilbert, who compiled a 10–5 record in Davis Cup competition between 1986 and 1993.

(5) Start the racket about 1 foot above where you'll be meeting the ball so that you can brush down the back of the ball with your strings to create backspin. Backspin slows the ball's forward motion when it hits the court, resulting in a short second bounce. "If the ball pops up in the air [your opponent] has an easy put-away shot."

(6) To create backspin, open the racket face by turning your forearm slightly clockwise, as if you are turning a key in a door. Stay low by bending your knees. Hit the underside of the ball with a slice shot so that the ball is on its way down as it is crossing the net. Gilbert says the ideal drop shot will clear the net by about 2 feet and bounce at least three times before rolling to the service line.

(7) Contact the ball in front of your body, between your shoulders and knees. Keep your elbow straight during contact with the ball and while finishing the shot. After contact, continue moving your racket toward the target area with a smooth and natural follow-through. "Don't choke the shot," says Gilbert.

(8) Try to hit a drop shot in the service box farthest from your opponent. Never hit a drop shot in the middle of the court. Whenever possible, Gilbert recommends hitting a drop shot behind your opponent so he will have to stop and change direction.

(9) The drop shot is a risky play, says Gilbert, because it requires split-second timing and perfect form. "You can look really stupid when you have the whole court open and then hit [a drop shot] into the net."

Brad Gilbert coached Andre Agassi to six Grand Slam singles titles and Andy Roddick to his only Slam triumph to date.

Nailing a Volley Winner

WAYNE BRYAN

Three-time WTT Coach of the Year

Continue to move forward as you hit the ball.

① Hold the racquet comfortably in your hand so you can volley using the same grip on both the forehand and backhand. Some coaches suggest holding the racket like you're shaking hands with it. "But there's no perfect way to [grip] it," says Bryan. "Experiment [with your grip] until you are confident hitting volleys off either side."

② When it comes to volleying, less is more. Keep your backswing short. Start with a stable base and turn your shoulders perpendicular to the net. Your racket should only go as far back as your shoulder turn takes it. To hit the volley, step forward and make contact out in front of you. Use a short, punching swing. "The power of the volley comes from the pace of the ball from your opponent rebounding off your racket strings," says Bryan, winner of the World Team Tennis Coach of the Year award for three consecutive seasons from 2004 to 2006.

③ Proper footwork is important to keep your volleys out of the net. "Don't wait for the ball to come to you [when volleying]," says Bryan. Move toward the ball and plant your front foot so it's lined up behind the eventual contact point. Don't stop your forward momentum before you make contact; that will close the racket face and cause a downward swinging motion. "Continue to move forward as you hit the ball."

④ Keep a firm wrist at the point of contact and finish with the racket head open at a 45-degree angle and pointed toward the target. "Your racket should follow through the line of the ball," says Bryan. Always keep your eyes on the ball. "Keep your focus on the shot rather

than on your opponent's movements." Keep your head steady and your chin down as you watch the ball hit the center of your racket strings.

⑤ On balls below the net, bend at the knees, not at the waist, and keep a straight upper body. "Don't bend your back when hitting a low volley," says Bryan, who coached the Sacramento Capitals to the World Team Tennis championship in 2002 and 2007. "Open your racket face to get the ball up and over the net."

⑥ To hit a backhand volley, start out in the ready position with good balance and knees bent. Take your racket back by turning your shoulders while stepping forward with your front foot at the same time. This allows your hips and shoulders to be sideways to the net, which puts you in line with the intended target. "The backhand volley is like throwing a karate chop," says Bryan. "Use a short backswing and take an aggressive step forward. The more aggressive you are with your feet on the volley, the more force you'll get on the shot."

⑦ To hit a proper backhand volley, plan to make contact with the ball about 18 inches out in front of your body with a firm wrist and follow through toward your target for a deeper volley. Push off with your back leg to propel your weight forward through the shot. As you make contact with the ball, keep your wrist locked and maintain a firm grip on the racket. On the follow-through, throw your opposite arm back to help maintain balance.

⑧ The backhand volley is a tough shot to master, says Bryan, because the back of your hand is facing the oncoming ball and the tips of your fingers are behind the racket. "You don't have a lot of support [on the racket handle] on impact," he says. "This can lead to a weak wrist, causing your elbow to pop out, which makes your [backhand] volley a floater for an easy put away [by your opponent]."

⑨ A player's volley is only as good as the approach shot leading up to it. "The harder and deeper [the approach shot], the better," says Bryan. Putting your opponent on the defensive will allow you to get closer to the net and give you better opportunities to end the point with a winning volley. "The closer you are to the net, the higher the volley, the easier it will be to hit a winner," says Bryan. Volley deep into the open court or angle the ball away from your opponent.

 Wayne Bryan coaches the world's number-one-ranked men's doubles team, his twin sons, Bob and Mike. The Bryan brothers have won seven career Grand Slam doubles titles.

Choosing the Right Bowling Ball

CHRIS BARNES
Two-time Bowler of the Year

The correct weight and finger fit are key.

① Find a ball that is the right weight for you. How? Start with a ball that is equal to one pound for every year of your age. For example, if you're ten years old, try a 10-pound ball. "This works until about age sixteen," says Barnes, the 2007 and 2008 Professional Bowlers Association player of the year.

② Put your fingers into the ball and let it hang at your side. "If the ball tilts your body, it's too heavy," says Barnes. Find the next-lightest ball. Repeat the hanging test until you find a ball that allows you to keep your shoulders square.

③ Next, check the distance between the top two holes and the thumbhole. "You should be able to slide your fingers into the ball up to the second knuckle and have your palm almost flat against the ball," he says.

④ Finally, work on finger fit. The sides of your fingers should lightly brush the edges of the holes. Says Barnes: "If you have to 'knuckle' the ball to hold on to it, the holes are too big."

⑤ To bowl, start four or five steps behind the foul line. If you're right-handed, walk so that you finish with your left foot forward. (Lefties should do the opposite.) "This gives you balance," he says. On your last step, slide forward on your front foot. Keep your trailing leg on the ground as long as possible. "That keeps your body centered," says Barnes, the 1998 PBA Rookie of the Year.

⑥ After you insert the thumb, middle, and ring fingers of your bowling hand into the ball, bring the ball back alongside your body. "The

straighter you can keep your arm [as you bring the ball back], the better," says Barnes. "Once you start pushing the ball [forward], gravity takes over. Don't try to force anything, let the ball come off your hand naturally." Now, knock 'em down.

Chris Barnes is the winner of twelve career PBA titles, including two majors: the 2005 U.S. Open and the 2006 Tournament of Champions.

Executing a Proper Billiards Break

EWA LAURANCE
Billiards Hall of Famer

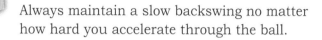

Always maintain a slow backswing no matter how hard you accelerate through the ball.

① Place the cue ball along the head string line about 12 to 14 inches from the side rail. Always be certain you are given a tight rack, says Laurance, "so the balls explode on impact. A loose rack is a dud rack."

② Before you get into position to shoot, bend slightly at the waist and put your bridge hand down about 8 inches from the cue ball. For a stable break-shot stance, distribute your body weight evenly on each leg about shoulder-width apart. Stand more erect to break than for a regular shot, "so you can get your body into it and your [shooting] arm can clear your hip," she says.

③ Face the shot. Laurance suggests a player line up the break shot by forming an imaginary line from the cue ball through the head ball to the rail. In your stance, a right-handed player should turn his body to the right at about a 45-degree angle to the shot. Place the tip of your right toe directly under the line of the cue stick. Your left toe should be slightly to the left side of the aim line. (Left-handed players should do the opposite.)

④ Hold the cue stick comfortably with the thumb and first three fingers. When the cue stick is gripped properly, it should not touch the palm of your hand. "Have a loose grip on the cue at all times," says Laurance. When you are in the shooting position, your shooting hand should be directly under your elbow.

⑤ Slightly bend both knees so your weight can be easily transferred toward the shot on the follow-through. Avoid the temptation to drive

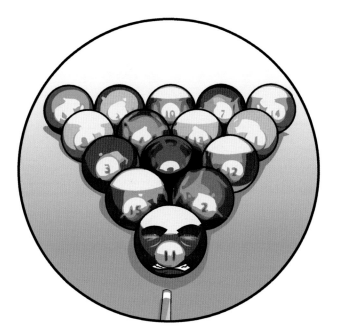

the cue ball through the rack. Always maintain a slow backswing no matter how hard you accelerate through the ball. "Never go back faster just because you want to shoot harder," says Laurance, who was inducted in the Billiards Congress of America Hall of Fame in 2004.

⑥ Aim the cue ball for the center of the head ball in the rack. After you've aimed, lock your eyes on the target, then after a slow backswing, use a smooth, direct stroke and hit the cue ball at or just above the center. "Hit the head ball as full as possible with a straight-on shot," says Laurance. A full hit will transfer all the cue ball's energy to the rack of balls.

⑦ It is imperative that your head remain perfectly still during the shot. Don't lunge at the cue ball or push off your back foot, because you'll lose control of the cue stick. Control is essential to an effective break, so only use the amount of power you can control. "Concentrate on the [proper] follow-through and not on power," says Laurance, the holder of multiple World and U.S. Open 9-Ball and 8-Ball titles. Keep the cue stick level as you follow through to maintain accuracy.

⑧ It is important that the cue tip strikes the cue ball a little above center, never to the left or right. Hit the cue ball high, to create topspin to keep forward momentum on the cue ball after it makes impact with the racked balls. This will give you a good break and set you up for the next shot.

 Ewa Laurance is the International and World Cup Trick Shot Champion.

Build a Solid Bridge

A solid bridge is an important yet often overlooked fundamental. If the shot is to be accurate, the bridge must be natural, yet give firm guidance to the cue.

Place your entire bridge hand flat on the table, about 8 inches behind the cue ball. The heel of your hand should be down firmly. Bend your index finger so that its tip touches your thumb, forming a loop.

Place the cue tip in the loop formed by your index finger and thumb, resting the cue against the inner groove of these two fingers. Extend the cue through the loop formed by your fingers.

Now pull your index finger firmly against the cue, but with the loop just loose enough so that you can stroke the cue back and forth easily. As you do this, keep your middle, ring, and pinkie fingers spread out and firmly pressed against the table. They form the bridge tripod, which must be firm yet natural.

You have the correct bridge when the cue passes through easily, accurately, and with firm guidance and support. The heel of your hand should be firmly on the table at all times. The bridge hand must not move while you are striking the ball.

Using a Mechanical Bridge

EWA LAURANCE
Billiards Hall of Famer

Quick Tip

Be careful not to bump the surrounding balls.

① If a shot is beyond your reach, or when you cannot comfortably stroke and follow through, use a mechanical bridge. "Don't sacrifice a shot because you can't use a [mechanical] bridge," says Laurance. "It's easy to learn."

② Set the bridge on the table 8 inches from the cue ball. Be sure to lay the bridge flat on the table if possible and secure it with your non-shooting hand. Place your palm atop the bridge to hold it down firmly. "Be careful not to bump the surrounding balls," says Laurance, a two-time player of the year. Flip the bridge on its side if the cue ball is blocked and you are forced to shoot over another ball.

③ Place the shaft of your cue on a grooved notch of the bridge. Place the cue in the slot that allows you to strike the cue ball with the cue as level as possible and in the place on the cue ball you wish to strike. Laurance recommends using the upper notch for *follow* and the lower side notches for *draw*.

④ Grasp the cue toward the end with your shooting hand. Place your thumb under the cue stick and your four fingers over the top of the cue. "Hold the stick lightly in your stroke hand," says Laurance, the 1991 women's Professional Billiards Association national champion. Bend your elbow so your forearm is horizontal to the table.

⑤ Face the shot standing upright. Aim by looking straight down your cue stick. You can get a great view down the length of the cue to the object ball. Laurance makes sure her chin is in line with the cue stick.

"Adjust [your aim] by moving the bridge, not [by moving] your shooting hand," she says.

⑥ As you prepare to stroke, your elbow will be sticking out to the side; the bridge will be to the left if you are right-handed. "A big mistake made by players is moving their elbow up and down," says Laurance. Strike the cue ball with a firm stroke and "follow through down toward the cloth [to avoid scratching]," she says. Immediately lift the bridge and cue off the table.

⑦ Practice using a mechanical bridge. Once you see how easily you can aim and pocket balls, you may never again want to shoot without a bridge.

Ewa Laurance holds the high run world record of 68 balls in women's competitive straight pool, set at the 1992 U.S. Open.

Throwing a Bulls-eye Dart

STEVE BROWN
Darts Hall of Famer

Quick Tip

Aim with your throwing arm, not your eyes.

① Pick up a dart and hold it, experimenting with different finger placements, until the dart feels well balanced in your hand. "A good grip is whatever is comfortable, whatever feels natural," says Brown, who was inducted into the U.S. National Darts Hall of Fame in 1997. Most players grip the dart between their thumb and index finger, using the other fingers to stabilize the dart.

② In darts, there is no actual right or wrong stance. "There's just better and worse ways," says Brown, currently ranked number one by the American Darts Organization. You want a solid stance, so your body doesn't move when you throw the dart. He recommends standing side-on, at a 45-degree angle to the target. Right-handed players should stand with their right foot forward; left-handed players should lead with their left foot. Lean forward slightly to keep your weight on your front foot, and use your back leg for balance. "Don't bend from the waist," says Brown, who turned pro in 1990. "Lean your whole body forward."

③ Don't aim the dart. "A dart doesn't go where you aim it, it goes where you throw it," says Brown. Accuracy comes with consistency and precision, not how you line up your eye with the dart and the target. "Aim with your arm, not your eyes," says Brown. "Once you have developed good [throwing] mechanics, [accuracy] comes down to feel, so you can throw the dart on the same plane [every time]."

④ When you throw a dart, movement should be isolated to your throwing arm. "The more you do [mechanically], the more there is to go wrong," says Brown. Think of your elbow as a hinge and your upper arm

as a lever. Keep your upper arm rigid and parallel to the floor. During the throwing motion, the only movement occurs from your elbow to your wrist.

⑤ Keep your elbow in a fixed position when moving the dart backward. Move the dart back as far as possible. Many professionals bring the dart back to their face, but Brown brings it back even farther, to the side of his ear. The backward movement should be smooth and fluid, with only a slight hesitation before beginning the forward stroke. "Go back gently and in one motion accelerate through the release of the dart."

⑥ Try to keep your wrist steady during the smooth backward movement, but snap your wrist as you release the dart. "The power comes from the wrist action," says Brown. After you've thrown your dart, hold your arm position for a moment. Your throwing hand should be aiming at the target, with your fingers extended. "A good follow-through will help your aim," says Brown.

⑦ When a dart flies, it travels not on a pure horizontal plane but along a parabolic curve. The best throwing technique takes this into account. Release the dart with the point tip up ever so slightly to allow the dart to travel along the parabolic curve. A dart that points down will result in a poor, wobbly throw. "If your forward stroke is accurate and you have a good release, that's all you need," says Brown.

 Steve Brown is the only American darter to hold all three national titles simultaneously, winning cricket, 501, and national ranking championships in 1998 and 1999.

Spinning on Ice Skates

ELAINE ZAYAK
Figure Skating Hall of Famer

Quick Tip

Stand tall as you spin.

① Stand still with your weight on the balls of your feet. Bend your knees. Keep your head up and your back straight. Extend both arms out to your side just below shoulder level.

② Push against the ice with your right foot so that you start moving in a circle around your left foot. Stop pushing and pull your right foot closer to your left. Press your left foot down so that the middle of your skate blade is on the ice. "Keep your left arm in front of your body and pull your right arm into your left [arm]," says Zayak, who was elected to the U.S. Figure Skating Hall of Fame in 2003. "Move your arms and legs together at the same time."

③ As you spin, Zayak says to form a circle with your arms at chest level "like you were hugging a favorite doll." Grasp one hand with the other and pull both hands toward your chest.

④ Stand tall as you spin, with your weight balanced over both feet. "You'll spin better on the middle of your [skate] blades," says Zayak, the 1982 World Figure Skating Champion. Don't lock your knees. Keep them slightly bent. Your feet should now be about 4 inches apart. "You gain speed in the spin because gravity is pulling against you."

⑤ To slow down and stop, extend your arms away from your body. Lean forward on your toe picks. (There are toe picks on the front of both skates. The picks have zigzag teeth to grip the ice.) Says Zayak: "Beginners won't be able to spin fast enough to get dizzy, but if you worry about becoming dizzy after a big spin, look straight ahead and keep your chin up to help the dizziness go away."

⑥ If you feel yourself beginning to fall, Zayak suggests bending your knees so you fall forward onto your side.

Elaine Zayak was the sixth-place finisher at the 1984 Sarajevo Winter Olympic Games.

Skating a Forward Crossover

ELAINE ZAYAK
Figure Skating Hall of Famer

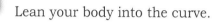

Lean your body into the curve.

① The forward crossover move lets you skate a curve. It is called a crossover because you "cross" one foot over the other. (These directions are for a right crossover. Switch the words *left* and *right* to do a left crossover.)

② The secret to doing anything on the ice is to keep your balance. To do so, stand with your weight on the balls of your feet. Bend your knees. "Always keep your knees slightly bent," says Zayak, the 1981 U.S. National Figure Skating Champion. "If your knees are stiff and locked, you're going to fall."

③ Keep your head up and your back straight. Don't let your arms swing behind you. If you do, you'll fall backward. "Lead with your left arm," says Zayak. "Keep your left arm in front of you and your right arm out to your side in an L position."

④ Glide forward on both feet. Push off with your right foot. As you glide on your left foot, bring your right foot forward and cross it over your left foot. "You are crossing over in line with your arms," says Zayak, the 1979 Girls' Junior World Champion.

⑤ Shift your weight from your left foot to the inside of your right foot. Lean your body into the curve. Push your left leg backward, stroking the ice under your right foot.

⑥ Bring both feet back to a side-by-side position to start again. "Push or pump your right foot, then cross the right [foot] over your left [foot], and end with your feet together," says Zayak. "Stand as if you are ready to march."

⑦　To help improve your skating, Zayak recommends taking lessons. Many rinks offer group lessons for beginners. If you really like skating, think about taking private lessons. Many competitive skaters also study dance to learn how to move on the ice with style. Says Zayak: "Don't worry if your skating looks a little rough at first. That's okay. Grace comes with practice and maturity."

Elaine Zayak placed fourth at the 1994 U.S. Championships and was named an alternate for the Olympic Games.

Swimming the Breaststroke

REBECCA SONI
Olympic Gold Medalist

Extend your arms and push them outward in a circular motion.

①　Of all the strokes used in swimming competition, the breaststroke seems to be the most relaxing. "It's not any easier [than other strokes], but it's at a more relaxed pace," says Soni, the gold medalist in the women's 200-meter breaststroke at the 2008 Summer Olympics. "Everything your hands and feet are doing is happening underneath the water, so you don't see all that's going on."

②　In competition, swimmers in breaststroke events dive off raised starting platforms at the sound of the starting gun. The swimmer floats on his stomach, with the legs bent slightly. The arms begin outstretched, with the hands almost touching, and push outward from each other in a circular motion. At the same time, the knees are brought toward the chest and then kicked outward in a frog kick. The process is then repeated. The swimmer breathes when the hands are pushed down to the sides of the body.

③　Breaststroke competition is contested at 100 and 200 meters. At 50 meters, the swimmer will be required to make a turn in order to swim back the other way. Quick turns can make the difference between first place and last place. Breaststroke swimmers use an open turn. They keep their heads above water while making the turn.

④　Use the frog kick when swimming the breaststroke. To start, the legs are fully extended and the toes are pointed toward the rear. "It's very important when you glide to be streamlined so you aren't dragging any water," says Soni, who also won 2008 Olympic silver medals in the

women's 100-meter breaststroke and the 4 × 100 medley relay. The heels are then pulled toward the hips just under the water's surface. "Keep your ankles flexed, so you can catch the water with your feet as you're kicking."

⑤ When the feet are near the hips, the knees are slightly bent and extended outward. Then, without pausing, the feet are pushed backward and the legs are pulled together until the toes point to the rear. Says Soni: "It's a similar action to the way a frog kicks its feet in the water."

Rebecca Soni won a breaststroke gold medal in the 100-meter competition and a silver medal in the 50 meters at the 2009 World Championships in Rome.

Punching a Speed Bag

ANGELO DUNDEE
Hall of Fame Boxing Trainer

Quick Tip

Hit the bag with the outside of your fist, not your knuckles.

① The speed bag should be positioned at a height that enables you to look directly at the middle of the bag. "Eye level is perfect," says Dundee, who was inducted into the International Boxing Hall of Fame in 1994. You'll have a hard time reaching the bag if it's hanging too high, and it will be tough to get underneath the bag if it's hanging too low.

② Face the bag straight on with your feet spread comfortably apart. "You're not in a boxing stance," says Dundee, best known for spending twenty-one years in Muhammad Ali's corner. "Don't point your shoulder; your chest is [square] to the bag." Keep your knees bent and your body loose and relaxed.

③ Always make sure to keep your hands up at chin level. This is the foundation of all proper boxing technique and enables you to punch the speed bag most efficiently. If your hands are held low, you will have to move your arms farther to hit the bag, throwing off your timing. "The speed bag is all about timing," says Dundee. "It sharpens your reflexes and improves your hand–eye coordination."

④ Make a fist with both hands. Point your elbows to the floor. The inside of your fists face each other sideways, so your knuckles are facing out. Aim to hit the bag directly in the center of the round belly of the bag so that it recoils true off your fist and flies straight back at you. "Always try to hit the same spot [on the bag]," says Dundee, who trained fifteen world champions, including Ali, Sugar Ray Leonard, Jimmy Ellis, and Carmen Basilio.

⑤ Hit the speed bag by pushing the back side of your fist into the bag in a straight motion. You should hit the bag with the outside of your fist, not with your knuckles. "Gently rap the bag with the back side of your hand," says Dundee. Your hand will pass through the bag and then downward and back. Follow through, keeping your wrist locked.

⑥ Do two right-hand punches in a row. Then do two left-hand punches in a row. "The timing of the rhythm is Right 1-2, Left 3-4," says Dundee. You do not have to hit the bag very hard. "It's not about force. It's strictly rhythm and hand–eye coordination." Go slow at first. Once you've developed a rhythm and honed your reflexes, then try a more advanced technique of making many repeated punches in quick succession on the bag.

⑦ After putting together a series of repeated strikes, you are ready to try the machine-gun technique. Punch the bag with your lead hand.

Position your other hand a few inches behind your lead hand. After the lead hand passes through the bag, immediately replace the lead hand with the other hand, striking the bag again. Move your fists in a continuous circle so they are rolling over one another. Continue replacing hands after you strike the bag, and you will soon begin to hear the rat-a-tat sound of a machine gun. That's when you know you're hitting the speed bag like Rocky Balboa.

 Angelo Dundee's last world champion was George Foreman, winner of the heavyweight title in 1994.

Kicking like Bruce Lee

ERICH KRAUSS
Professional Muay Thai Fighter

Muay Thai kicks and punches can be dangerous. Do not practice kicking or hitting other people without supervision by a qualified instructor.

① In martial arts, athletes punch and kick. But in Muay Thai the kicks are the most important weapons. "Muay Thai is like kickboxing," says Krauss, who has trained and fought in Thailand. "Most of the attack moves are kicks." Two of the most powerful kicks in Muay Thai are the roundhouse kick and the side kick.

② For the roundhouse kick, begin in the fighting stance. This stance is the starting position for all martial arts sparring moves. From this position, you can make quick moves with your hands and feet in any direction.

③ Stand with your feet parallel, about shoulder-width apart. Make fists with both hands. Hold them at chest level. "Keep your weight equally balanced on both legs," says Krauss. "Don't lean too far forward or backward."

④ From the fighting stance, lift your kicking (rear) foot up in front of you. Straighten your leg as you swing your foot around toward the target. Turn your hips into the kick. This will shift your weight into the kick and add power. Extend your leg fully, and strike the target with the instep of your foot. (The instep is the arched middle part of the foot between the toes and ankle.) "Snap your foot toward the target," says Krauss, the author of more than twenty-five books on the martial arts.

⑤ For the side kick, begin in the fighting stance. Pivot sideways on your non-kicking foot. Shift your hips forward slightly as you bend your knee to your chest and get ready to kick in front of you.

⑥ Turn your kicking foot so that the bottom of your heel is aimed at your opponent. Straighten your leg and drive your heel toward your opponent. Says Krauss: "In the roundhouse kick, the power comes from turning your hips. In the side kick, the power comes from shooting your leg out."

Erich Krauss is the author, most recently, of *Muay Thai Unleashed.*

Juggling Three Balls in the Air

JON KOONS
Juggling Jester and Instructor, JestMaster Academy,
New York Renaissance Faire

Practice while standing next to your bed with your knees against the mattress so you won't have to bend down so much when the balls drop, which will happen often while you're learning!

①　Stand in a comfortable position with your feet shoulder-width apart. Keeping your elbows at your sides and raise your hands so they are parallel to the ground. "Stay relaxed," says Koons. "Basic three-ball juggling is actually pretty easy, but just like any other [skill], it takes practice."

②　Start by holding one ball in your right hand. Imagine a string connecting your hands, and also imagine a box that is open just above your head. Toss the ball underhand into the corner of the imaginary box over your left hand. Let the ball drop into your left hand. Then toss the ball back to your right hand in the same way. Keep your hands parallel to the ground. The ball should drop into your hand without your having to reach out to make the catch. "Remember: you are throwing side to side, not forward or backward," says Koons.

③　When practicing the underhand toss, Koons recommends "popping" the ball out of your hand with your palm instead of moving your entire arm. "This will give you better control and prevent the ball from rolling forward off your fingers," he says. Practice tossing one ball from hand to hand until you can "pop" the ball into the imaginary box

corners back and forth and catch it every time. When you succeed at this you are ready to add a second ball.

④ Hold one ball in each hand. Now, when you toss the ball into a corner of the imaginary box you will have to get rid of the ball already in your other hand before you can catch the one you've just tossed. "The trick is learning when to do that," says Koons. "There is a split second between the time the ball you've tossed stops going up and when it starts to come down. That's [the precise instant] when you toss the ball already in your hand into the opposite box corner. If you aim for those box corners the balls should drop into your hands right on target."

⑤ Make sure to be consistent with your toss. Don't throw the balls too high or too low. "Take your time," says Koons. "Don't rush or try to throw the balls at the same time. Always wait for the first ball to start dropping before tossing the second [ball]." To help fine-tune your timing,

Koons suggests verbalizing the movements as you go along. "If you say out loud, 'Toss, toss, catch, catch' or count 'one, two' for the tosses and 'three, four' for the catches, it will help to get your timing right." Practice tossing the balls back and forth and catching them every time. Once you can do this confidently you are ready to add a third ball.

⑥ Hold two balls in one hand and one ball in the other hand. Always begin your toss with the hand holding two balls. Don't worry about throwing the third ball just yet. Continue to practice tossing just two balls back and forth, while keeping the third ball in your hand just to get the feel of catching a ball while still holding another ball. Once you can do this and catch the ball every time you can add the third ball into the tossing pattern.

⑦ Just because you've added a third ball into the tossing pattern doesn't change the basic juggling concept. "Any time a ball is falling toward a hand that already has a ball in it, toss the ball in that hand so you can catch the ball [that's falling]," says Koons. Continue to use your timing mechanism. "For your tosses count 'one, two, three' and the catches will take care of themselves." Practice until you can catch each ball every time. "Now you're juggling!" says Koons. "It's just a matter of keeping the pattern going."

⑧ Practice makes perfect, so keep at it. "Don't be discouraged when you drop a ball," says Koons. "The main thing is to relax and have fun." Each time you practice, start with one ball, then two, then three, to get back into the rhythm. Keep the balls in the air as long as you can. Soon you'll be juggling like a pro!

Jon Koons was named New York City's Plum Craziest Performer in a national talent search. He has performed magic, clowning, ventriloquism, stilt walking, fire-eating, juggling, and mime across the United States and around the world.

Outdoor Fun and Games

Landing a Kick Flip on a Skateboard

BUCKY LASEK
X Games Gold Medalist

Stay over the board as you are jumping.

① A kick flip is an intermediate-level trick in which the skater turns over the board while doing an Ollie. To execute a clean kick flip, the skater flips the board over at least once while jumping in the air, and then lands squarely on the board, wheels down, and rides it out. Before you try one, you should already be comfortable doing an Ollie.

② To set up for a kick flip, position your back foot on the center of the tail of your board. The ball of your front foot should be near the middle of the board and just behind the bolts of your front truck, with your toes pointed slightly toward the nose. Find a stance that feels comfortable. "Go with what feels best on your feet," says Lasek, winner of ten X Games medals in skateboard vert, including six gold medals.

③ Press down with your back foot to smack the tail of the board on the ground, as you would for an Ollie, then jump up in the air. The harder you snap your tail and jump, the higher your board will soar.

④ Once you're up in the air and your board is flipping, Lasek says it's important not to push down on the board, "so you get big air." Stay over the board as you're jumping. This allows you to control the trick on the way down. "Make sure to stay directly over the board," he says. "A lot of kids kick the board away from them."

⑤ To make the board spin underneath you while you're in the air, use the outside of your front foot and drag it, while scraping the heel-side edge of your board to make it spin around. The harder you kick off your front foot, the faster the board will spin. Make sure to use the top of your toes and not the bottom of your foot. "Flick [the board with] your ankle for maximum pop," says Lasek, winner of the 2008 X Games gold medal for Best Trick.

⑥ Land with your feet as close to the bolts as possible. Bend your knees when you hit the ground. "When you're learning, you want to land on the board any way you can, but having your feet land on top of the bolts of your board is a very good spot to aim for," says Lasek.

⑦ It's also a good idea to practice on a carpet to prevent your board from slipping out from under you. "You're going to mess up in the beginning, but don't give up." With practice, you can pull off this trick and establish some street cred.

 Bucky Lasek became the first skateboarder in X Games history to win a gold medal in consecutive years (1999 and 2000); he repeated the feat in 2003–04.

Riding a Rail on a Skateboard

BUCKY LASEK
X Games Gold Medalist

Keep your board as flat as possible
on the rail.

① Riding a rail is a gnarly move. "It's a showcase trick," says Lasek, "but it's nowhere near easy to do." Lasek recommends learning the move on a low rail or ledge at first. "It's tough to get up on a high obstacle," he says. "Skateboarding is all mental. You've got to *know* that you can do it."

② Ride up to a rail at a comfortable approach speed. "Don't go straight at the rail, come in at a little bit of an angle," says Lasek, who turned pro in 1990. "I bend my knees and get a little hop [up to the rail] depending on how high it is."

③ Be sure that the nose of your board is going to clear the rail. You want to land with the rail in the middle of your board. Jump onto the rail with your board centered lengthwise over it. Jump as high as you can; that way, if you miss the rail, you'll have a chance to clear it.

④ Shift your shoulders and head so that they are positioned over your front foot. "Lock in to that position and balance. Keep your board as flat as possible [on the rail]. That will make it easier to slide."

⑤ To land on the rail, catch the board with your feet and push down on the rail. Let the board slide. Keep your body straight up for balance. "Make sure you're not leaning too far over your edge, or you'll slide right out," says Lasek, who, in 2004, won titles at the Vans Triple Crown, Gravity Games, and the Slam City Jam.

⑥ As you near the middle of the rail, focus your eyes on the end of the rail to help stay balanced. Keep your board centered over the rail

the entire time. "The only time you can get into problems is when you let your edge touch the rail," says Lasek.

⑦ Once you're near the end of the rail, look down so you can spot your landing. Ride the rail to the end. Be patient. As you near the end of the rail, jump off and rotate your body 90 degrees so that you and your board come off straight. "You can hop off the rail or you can do a trick off the rail."

⑧ Bend your knees and crouch to absorb the impact of the landing. If you aren't able to ride to the end, a word of caution: Jump off the rail—don't turn off the rail. "The rail hurts," says Lasek.

Bucky Lasek was the first action sports athlete to appear on the cover of *ESPN The Magazine* (July 19, 2004).

Skiing Moguls

HEATHER McPHIE
2007 World Cup Rookie of the Year

Quick Tip

Always keep your shoulders facing downhill.

① You are standing at the top of the mogul run, contemplating your line down the slope. "Don't expect to find the perfect zipper line," says McPhie, a moguls racer with the U.S. Freestyle Ski Team. "Find a narrow path to go through and keep your skis pointing straight down the hill."

② A good mogul skier remembers to always keep his eyes up. Once you've started skiing, don't look down at your skis or at the moguls beneath you. Focus several moguls ahead and concentrate on your line. "Don't look down, because that always ends badly," says McPhie, who competed in her first World Cup moguls competition in 2006.

③ Ski the tops of the bumps for a gentler ride. Don't hop from mogul to mogul. Make quick turns on the balls of your feet. When turning, keep your shoulders facing downhill and your upper body still. Twist at your hips to make the skis turn. Ski on a hard edge and keep pressure on your skis as you are turning.

④ Keep your hands in front of your body to stay forward as you travel downhill. Plant your pole at the top of the mogul and rotate around the pole. "Stay centered over your skis and lead with your core," says McPhie. For better balance and control, try to keep your knees directly over your feet and your hips directly over your bindings. "If you lean back, your skis get too far out in front [of you] and you'll lose control."

⑤ Try to keep your skis in contact with the snow as long as possible. "Roll off the back side of one mogul into the next one," says McPhie, who took fourth place at the 2008 World Cup Finals. Absorb the oncoming bump when your ski tips hit the snow. Use your knees like springs to absorb the impact. "Relax your body, and don't feel nervous," she says. "Don't stiffen or be tense."

⑥ At first, moguls skiing can seem intimidating. "Be willing to make two turns and be excited about it," says McPhie. "That's an awesome start. Next time, plan the bumps so you can try for three turns." Link together as many turns as you can before resting. "Try finding a rhythm, but don't force things. Try to flow [downhill] at a steady pace."

Fast Fact Heather McPhie was the 2005 and 2006 NorAm Grand Prix moguls champion.

Surfing the Perfect Wave

STEPHANIE GILMORE
Two-time Women's World Titleholder

Standing up on the board is a difficult skill, but knowing *when* to stand up is also important.

① Every wave is different. But catching a wave is all about timing. "It's about finding the perfect moment to pop up [on your board]," says Gilmore, winner of the 2007 and 2008 Association of Surfing Professionals Women's World Title. "Get up too quickly and then you don't catch the wave. Get up too late and you'll fall off the back of the wave."

② To start, lie down on your board in the prone position (on your stomach) and paddle out to sea. Paddle out beyond the breaking waves. "Make sure the tip of the nose [of the board] is a little longer than an arm's length in front of you," says Gilmore, an Aussie who took up surfing at age ten. Wait for a good-looking wave, keeping the nose of your board pointed slightly out of the water, so you can easily pivot the board in any direction to catch that perfect wave.

③ When you see an appealing wave approach, spin around until the nose of your board is pointing in the direction of the wave. Paddle hard in the same direction as the force of the wave. Position yourself near the peak of the wave, where the wave is highest and will break first. "Go where the wave is opening," says Gilmore. "Then paddle straight down the face of the wave." Don't stop paddling until you feel the wave pick you up and propel you and your board forward.

④ When you have paddled into position, and the wave is propelling you forward, prepare to pop up to your feet. Grab the sides of the

surfboard (the rails) at a level between your shoulders and your chest. When you feel the wave is picking you up, use your arms and knees to push your body up toward the nose of the board and quickly pull your legs up beneath you. "Do a one-motion push-up from the rails," says Gilmore. "Use your knees to help pitch yourself up."

⑤ The key to popping up is to remember to squat first and then stand up. Keep your hands on the board until your feet can get into position. To do so, you'll need to stay in a low crouch or squatting position. "Keep your butt down," says Gilmore, who won her first event, the 2005 Roxy Pro Gold Coast, at age seventeen. "Bend at your knees rather than your hips." Gilmore recommends practicing pop-ups on your board while still on the beach. Lay your board on the sand and practice pushing up and popping to your feet. When you pop up, try to plant your feet in the riding position, so you won't have to make adjustments. "Make sure the fins are facing down [to the sand]."

⑥ Standing up on the board is a difficult skill, but knowing *when* to stand up is also important. There is a critical moment to catch a wave and stand up. Just when you feel you and the wave are traveling at the same speed, jump from a prone to standing position before the wave breaks. "It's a strange sensation," says Gilmore. "When you feel the motion of the wave pick you up, that's when you know to jump to your feet." Do it fast, and plant your feet firmly on the board.

⑦ Quickly turn your body so your feet are perpendicular to the rails. Put your left foot forward if you're a regular-footed rider or your right foot forward if you're goofy. "Place your feet in the center of the board over the top of the stringer a little wider than shoulder-width apart," says Gilmore. "Be in a power stance and use your arms to help stay balanced."

⑧ Lean toward the wave-side rail and start riding the wave. "Ride it as long as you can." Keep your weight as far over the nose of the board as you can without dipping it under the water. Steer by using pressure from your back foot and by twisting your arms and hips.

 Stephanie Gilmore became the first rookie ever to claim the ASP Women's World Title.

Spiking a Volleyball

HOLLY McPEAK
Volleyball Hall of Famer

Quick Tip

Strike the ball with an open palm.

① A spike—jumping into the air and hitting the ball downward into the opponent's side of the court—is an explosive offensive tactic. A successful spike will result in a *kill*, meaning a point scored for your team. Spiking requires a player to have excellent timing and jumping ability.

② Position yourself 1 or 2 feet from the net. Anticipate where your teammate is setting the ball so you can get into position to jump for the spike. Knowing exactly when to begin your jump comes with experience. "It's all in the timing, and timing is learned," says McPeak, a 2009 inductee into the Volleyball Hall of Fame. "As soon as you see where the ball is set, start your approach."

③ Use a three-step approach to generate height for your jump. Start with your left foot behind your right foot and take your first step with your left foot. (Left-handed hitters should do the opposite.) The objective of the first step is to build up momentum, so make this first step a strong one.

④ The second step is with your right foot, and this step will take you closer to the ball. The distance of the second step will vary depending on how much you need to adjust to the position of the ball in relation to the net. Take a long step if the ball is set close to the net and farther away from you; take a smaller step if the ball is set close to you and farther from the net.

⑤ As you take the second step, bend your knees to lower your body in preparation for the jump while simultaneously swinging your arms

behind you like a pendulum. Your arm swing will help you jump higher. Keep your head up and your eyes on the ball.

⑥ The final step is with your left foot, and it follows quickly after your second step. The aim of the final step is to gather your feet underneath you to control your body's momentum. Keep both feet shoulder-width apart to maintain balance.

⑦ At the instant your last step of the approach lands on the ground, start to jump off both feet. Keep your body slightly turned so that your hitting shoulder is pointing away from the net. Swing your hands forward and upward while pushing off with both legs to lift your body into the air; jumping this way helps you soar into the air and also begins to place your arms in the proper hitting position. "Make sure to swing your arms up high for upward momentum," says McPeak, a beach volleyball bronze medalist at the 2004 Olympic Games. It is important to jump as vertically as possible, because if any part of your body touches the net, you will be called for a net violation.

⑧ As you near the height of your jump, draw your hitting arm back behind your head as you rise. "Cock your elbow back like you're pulling a bow and arrow, with your elbow high," says McPeak, winner of seventy-two career beach volleyball titles, third best on the all-time list. Point your left hand at the ball, which helps you line it up in your sights. "Your left arm is up in the air while the right arm is swinging [back]."

⑨ Your hitting hand should be open and relaxed, with the palm slightly curved to the shape of the ball. "It's important that the ball be in your sights. The ball should be high and in front of your hitting shoulder so you can see the court and the ball [at the same time]." Make sure to contact the ball as high as possible above your hitting shoulder and slightly in front of your body. "Hit [the ball] squarely with the open palm of your hand," says McPeak, who turned pro in 1991. "The bigger the surface area the better, so a big open palm with fingers strong and wide open [works best]."

⑩ Strike the ball with an open palm, accelerating your hand toward the ball, and then snap your wrist down with a whipping action as you make contact with the ball to create topspin. "Come over the top of the ball to bring the ball down and into the court," says McPeak. The hitter's goal is either to place the ball where an opposing player is not or to hit the ball so hard that it cannot be returned. "Use your wrist and fingers to help control the ball. The ball is going to go where you tell it to go. If you want it to go down the line, just aim down the line." As your body descends to the ground, bend your knees and use your leg muscles to absorb the force of the landing and to regain your balance.

⑪ If you're not tall enough, or simply can't jump high enough to hit the ball when it's above the height of the net, you should spike farther away from the net whenever possible. "Still try to hit the ball forward and with topspin," says McPeak, "but don't snap your wrist down."

 Holly McPeak is a five-time Most Valuable Player in three different U.S. beach volleyball touring leagues.

Blowing Past a Lacrosse Defender

GARY GAIT
Lacrosse Hall of Famer

Make sure to keep the shaft of the stick straight up and down.

① When cradling the ball in the pocket of your stick, grip the shaft with the top part of your palms and keep your hands loose. Holding the stick with two hands, flex your wrists back and forth. You should get comfortable cradling with both your right and left hand on top. "You can't develop any other skills until you're comfortable cradling the ball. It

should be instinctive after a period of time," says Gait, who was inducted into the National Lacrosse Hall of Fame in 2005. When cradling with one hand, hold the stick near the top of the shaft and use the same wrist motion. Make sure to keep the shaft of the stick straight up and down.

② In lacrosse the move you use to get past a defender is called a *dodge*. The key is to make your opponent lean in the opposite direction of where you want to go. "If I want to go to my right, I want to lunge to the left and get the defender to bite, thinking I'm going left," says Gait, who scored 192 goals during his college career at Syracuse University from 1987 to 1990. "Then I shift my weight to the right and accelerate past him."

③ After you get past your defender, accelerate toward the goal at full speed. You should square your shoulders toward the goal and prepare to either shoot or pass. If you shoot overhand, aim low. If you shoot underhand, aim high. "The goalie is going to be following the head of your stick, and if the ball stays on the same plane [as your stick], he has a better chance of saving it," says Gait, currently coach of the Syracuse women's lacrosse team. "If the ball changes planes, it has a better chance of going in."

 Gary Gait is a seven-time league Most Valuable Player—six times in the National Lacrosse League (1995–99, 2003) and once in Major League Lacrosse (2005).

Riding a Bike with No Hands

SCOTTY CRANMER
X Games Gold Medalist

Learn to ride one-handed before moving on to no-hands riding.

① Put on your helmet, elbow pads, and knee pads for safety. Find some flat ground to ride on.

② Practice coasting with one hand off the handlebars. Begin pedaling. Keep your strong hand on the handlebars to hold them steady, and briefly take your other hand off the bars. Coast. Place your hand back on the handlebars whenever you feel the need.

③ Continue removing and replacing your hand until you feel safe enough to coast one-handed. Let your free arm hang by your side.

④ Work on pedaling while holding on with one hand. Start slowly at first. Move only your lower body. "You want to keep your [upper] body almost tense," says Cranmer, winner of two gold medals (2006 and 2009) and two silver medals (2005 and 2007) at the X Games in the BMX free-style park event.

⑤ Now practice coasting with no hands, using the same technique you used in steps 2 and 3. With one arm at your side, briefly remove the other hand from the handlebars. Replace it as you need to. Be sure to keep your body's weight back and over the seat.

⑥ Squeezing your knees in toward the seat will help you keep your balance. When you're ready, try pedaling with no hands. "If you're nervous, give it a few more days [one-handed]," says Cranmer. Once you've got the knack, go ahead and show off.

 Scotty Cranmer became the first BMXer ever to land a frontflip tailwhip in competition in 2007.

Putting a Worm on a Fish Hook

KEVIN VANDAM
Five-time BASS Angler of the Year

The hook does not hurt the worm.

① If you're nervous or scared about handling a worm, get comfortable with one first. "Get the feel of it wriggling around on your palm and touching you," says VanDam, who won the BASS Angler of the Year in 1992, 1996, 1999, 2008, and 2009.

② Grasp the worm near its head. Insert the hook into its body about three quarters of an inch below the head and push the hook all the way through the body.

③ Poke the hook through again a little below your first hole. Slide the worm up the shaft of the hook. Continue poking the hook through the body a little below each hole and sliding the worm up.

④ Leave the tail dangling from the hook. "Lively worms catch more fish," says VanDam.

Kevin VanDam is a two-time Bassmaster Classic champion (2001 and 2005).

Catching More Fish

KEVIN VANDAM
Five-time BASS Angler of the Year

 Make sure you learn the proper cast.

(1) To catch more fish, "make sure you learn to cast the right way," says VanDam, winner of the first Elite 50 championship in 2005. Casting is flicking the rod forward and releasing the line so the lure is thrown into the water. The distance and accuracy of a cast are the keys to making the baited hook land where fish are feeding.

(2) To cast, begin with the reel open. Hold the rod at the 2 o'clock position, pointing toward the target area of the lake or other body of water. Then bring the rod to the 12 o'clock position. Now push the rod

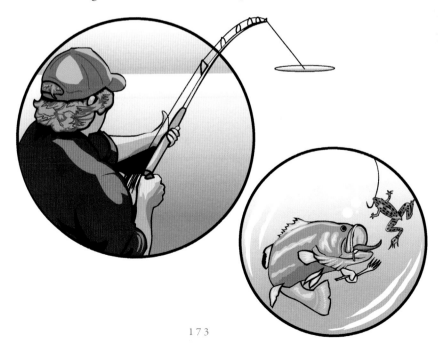

forward, stopping it at the 2 o'clock position, and release the line. The lure will shoot forward in an arc toward the water, pulling the line from the reel.

③ Lures, or artificial bait, are made from wood, plastic, and metal. Lures are designed to look and move like creatures fish normally eat. "The more experience you have [fishing], the better you'll know which lure to use," says VanDam, who was named Outdoor Sportsman of the Year by ESPN in 2002.

④ There are five types of lures: *plugs*, which float, sink, or dive rapidly; *spoons*, which wobble or flutter as they are pulled through the water by the line; *spinners*, which rotate and make vibrations; *jigs*, which sink to the bottom and then make short, quick hops as the line is reeled back; and *flies*, which often look like insects.

⑤ Fly fishing is a challenging way to catch freshwater fish. The most skilled anglers often tie their own flies out of such materials as thread, feathers, and hair. "[Freshwater fish] can spot fake bait, so the fly better look real," says VanDam.

Kevin VanDam has 14 B.A.S.S. first-place finishes since turning pro in 1990.

Skipping a Stone across Water

RUSSELL BYARS
Stone Skipping World Record Holder

The front lip of the stone should have an upward tilt when it hits the water.

① Skipping a stone across water requires three key elements: spin, angle, and speed. "And a good combination of the three," says Byars, who set a Guinness World Record by bouncing a stone fifty-one times. The stone traveled 250 feet across Pennsylvania's French Creek on July 19, 2007.

② First, find a stone that is flat and smooth on one side. Byars, forty-five, prefers rounded stones, about 3 to 4 inches across. Choose a stone you can throw comfortably. It should weigh about the same as a golf ball. "Lighter stones tend to curve," he says. "Heavier stones will sink."

③ Now find a calm section of water. Stand on land sideways to the water with your feet shoulder-width apart, like a pitcher in the stretch position. Hold the stone between your thumb and index finger. Curl the other fingers underneath so the stone is resting on them. "Make a fist and then extend your thumb and index finger to [form] a backward C if you're right handed," says Byars, who has been entering stone skipping competitions since 2002.

④ Firmly grip the stone. Byars favors a stone with a slight chip or divot at the point or on the side, "so my index finger can get in the notch and make the stone spin real [fast]."

⑤ Bend your knees, placing your weight on your back foot. Then step forward, bringing your arm above your head, and throw the stone sidearm as close to the water level as you can. Make sure to throw it low, like you are trying to slide it across the water. "Follow through and feel

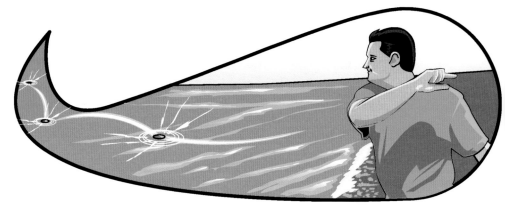

your index finger pushing on the stone," says Byars. "Snap your wrist to get the stone spinning as fast as possible."

⑥ Byars throws with a straight upper body, but most skippers bend over at the waist and lean way down on the release. Whatever your technique, the front lip of the stone should have an upward tilt when it hits the water. Downward tilt will result in a sinking stone. "Don't throw a submarine," he says.

⑦ How high above the water you release the stone will determine the angle of the stone hitting the water. "Apparently, the perfect angle for the stone to hit the water is 20 degrees," says the six-foot, two-inch, 253-pound right-hander. If your stone is bouncing high off the water, then you have too much angle and the stone is hitting the water too close to land.

⑧ Technique is more important than throwing speed. Throw the stone as fast as you can while still maintaining control of the stone's angle and spin. Says Byars: "The better the angle and spin, the more skips, regardless of speed."

Russell Byars started skipping stones for fun while walking his dog, Bear. He competes wearing a T-shirt that reads: SKIPS STONES FOR FUDGE.

Tossing a Frisbee

BART WATSON
Captain, U.S. National Ultimate Frisbee Team

The term Frisbee is used generically to describe all flying disks, but the name is a registered trademark of the Wham-O toy company.

① There are three common ways to throw a flying disk: backhand, sidearm, and overhand. "Most people throw backhand first because the mechanics are easiest to learn," says Watson.

② To throw backhand, curl your pinkie, ring, and middle fingers back against the rim under the inside edge of the disk. Place your index finger on the outside edge for stability and your thumb on top of the disk. You hold a flying disk to throw backhand pretty much the way you'd pick it up off the ground—and like the way you'd grab a fan to fan yourself. Once you've mastered this grip, Watson recommends curling your index finger underneath, too. "That will increase throwing accuracy," he says.

③ Stand sideways to where you want to throw, with your shoulders pointing 90 degrees from the target. You can stand in a karate-like stance with your back foot square and your front foot aimed at the target. Or you can stand straight up, feet shoulder-width apart, with the toes of both feet in an even line. "Bend your knees a little bit and find the most stable stance possible that is also the most comfortable," says Watson.

④ Start by extending your throwing arm toward the target. Bring your throwing arm back across your body, pulling the disk toward your non-throwing shoulder. "Cock your wrist back," says Watson. "Snapping your wrist is the most important part of throwing a Frisbee."

⑤ Take one step toward the target. (Right-handed throwers lead with the right foot.) As you bring your arm forward, snap your wrist just before you release the disk. Snapping your wrist causes the disk to rotate. "Spin is everything," says Watson. "The more spin, the more control." Release the disk when your arm is fully extended, at the point when your hand is in the center of your body. "You whip your arm forward to throw, but snapping your wrist is how you'll generate the most power."

⑥ To throw for distance, start by facing the target. Then turn your front throwing shoulder to the target at the same time you are stepping across your body with your front leg. (Right-handed throwers pivot on their left foot and step across their body with their right leg. Lefties do the opposite.) "Drive across your body to generate power from your hips," says Watson. Remember to always hold the disk parallel to the ground. "Releasing the Frisbee flat makes the disk stable and able to hold its line for a straighter, longer flight."

⑦ For tricks, tilt the outside edge up a bit to curve the flying disk from left to right; tilt the edge down slightly to curve from right to left. (The opposite is true for lefty throws.) If the disk spins sideways soon after releasing it, you are throwing too much with your shoulder and need more wrist and elbow snap in your throwing motion. Says Watson: "A problem kids have, because they are low to the ground, they lean back too much and throw the Frisbee up."

⑧ The top flying-disk players can toss a disk more than 400 feet. That's the distance from home plate to the center-field fence in many professional baseball stadiums. Don't worry about how far you can throw when you first start. Focus on throwing accurately over a short distance and then expand your field of play.

 Bart Watson and the U.S. National Ultimate Frisbee Team won the gold medal at the World Games in 2005 and 2009. Watson and the San Francisco Jam won the Ultimate Players Association Club Championship in 2008, and he was a member of the Stanford University squad that won the UPA College Championship in 2002.

Flying Saucers

There are two other common ways to throw a disk and five ways to catch one.

Sidearm Toss: Hold the disk with your thumb on top and your index and middle fingers below. Your wrist should be tilted backward. To throw, swing your arm down at about a 30- to 40-degree angle and snap your wrist forward. Watson says this is the most accurate method of throwing.

Overhand Toss: Hold the disk with your thumb underneath and fingers on top. Tilt your wrist backward. Swing your arm forward at shoulder level. Snap your wrist at the point of release.

Catches: There are five catches that can be used: between the legs, behind the head, behind the back, finger catch, and tipping. Tipping is when the Frisbee is tapped lightly in the center just before it is caught.

ACKNOWLEDGMENTS

This book would not have been possible without the creativity, sound judgment, and tireless work of my collaborators at Skyhorse Publishing. The scope of the book was greatly enhanced by the imagination of senior editor Mark Weinstein and the designers at Kryon Publishing Services. Many thanks to copy editor Susan Barnett and proofreader Julie Matysik for making me look good and for keeping me honest. Thanks also to Adam Wallenta, whose colorful illustrations brought words to life. Naturally, this project would have been difficult to complete without the understanding and support of my wife, Carolyn, and my children, Rachel and Jack. Finally, to Robert L. Fischer, the original cool sports dad. Many others contributed ideas, time, advice, and encouragement. They include league communications directors, team public relations managers, media relations coordinators, and player agents for helping to arrange the interviews, and, of course, to the athletes and coaches who took the time to speak with me. To all of them, and to numerous other friends and associates who shared my vision, my deep and abiding thanks.

ABOUT THE AUTHOR

Davto Fischer has written numerous books on sports for adults and young readers, including *Greatest Sports Rivalries*, *The 50 Coolest Jobs in Sports*, and *Do Curve Balls Really Curve?* He has written for the *New York Times* and *Sports Illustrated for Kids*, and has worked for *Sports Illustrated*, *NBC Sports*, and the *National Sports Daily*. He was presented a Distinguished Achievement Award for Excellence in Educational Publishing in 1998. David lives in River Vale, New Jersey, with his wife, Carolyn, and children, Rachel and Jack. He has been a cool sports dad for fifteen years.